I0017789

M 1 CHIP MAC MINI USER GUIDE

THE ULTIMATE BEGINNER'S MANUAL TO USING THE LATEST M 1 CHIP MAC MINI WITH TIPS AND TRICKS

BY

FELIX O. COLLINS

Copyright © 2021 FELIX O. COLLINS

All rights reserved. No part of this book shall be reproduced, stored in a retrieval system, or transmitted by any means, electronic, mechanical, photocopying, recording, or otherwise, without written permission from the publisher. Although every precaution has been taken in the preparation of this book, the publisher and author assume no responsibility for errors or omissions. Nor is any liability assumed for damages resulting from the use of the information contained herein.

LEGAL NOTICE:

This book is copyright protected and is only for personal use. This book should not be amended or distributed, sold, quote, or paraphrased without the consent of the author or publisher.

Contents

INTRODUCTION

Apple relaunched the Mac mini in November 2020 to launch low-end and mid-range models with the new M1 chip.

This is Apple's first major update to the Mac mini since October 2018. The new M1 model is on sale as well as the top 6-core Intel Core i5 chip model.

The M1 chip on the Mac mini is Apple's first program on the Mac chip, which includes GPU, CPU, RAM, and more to improve efficiency. The M1 on the Mac mini has an 8-core CPU with four high-performance and four cores, as well as an eight-core integrated GPU.

On the Mac mini, the CPU M1 chip provides three times the performance of the previous generation of entry-level models, while the GPU provides 6 times the graphics performance. With a 16-core neural engine, the machine learning load is 15 times faster, while the Mac mini is five times faster than the best-selling Windows desktop in its price range.

The Mac mini has never experienced any changes in its design and continues to use the one-piece single-piece flat chassis, 1.4-inch square. The M1 Mac mini has a silver version, while the Intel Mac mini has a gray space version.

Apple said the advanced temperature design of the M1 Mac mini keeps working while keeping the machine cool and quiet. It can be upgraded up to 16GB of RAM, and the Intel model can support up to 64GB. Both models can be upgraded to a larger 2TB storage space.

The M1 Mac mini supports a full 6K display and 4K display with HDMI, while the previous generation model supports up to 5K displays. Other features include WiFi 6, which supports faster WiFi speeds, and Secure Enclave for advanced security. The IM1 Mac mini has two Thunderbolt 3 / USB 4 ports, two USB-A ports, one HDMI 2.0 port, and Gigabit Ethernet ports.

The price for 8GB RAM and 256GB SSD with M1 Mac mini starts at $ 699, the model with 512GB SSD starts at $ 899, and the Intel Core model with 6-core 8th generation Intel Core i5 chip with UHD graphics 630 starting at $ 699. The price is the US $ 1,099.

Currently, consumers should postpone the use of the Intel-based Mac mini in early 2018/2020 until the performance difference between the Intel chip and the new Apple M1 chip becomes more apparent.

Mac mini at a glance

Take a tour of Mac mini

Note: This guide works on Mac mini currently using Apple M1 chip and Mac mini using Intel processor. This picture shows a Mac mini with an Apple M1 chip. If you're not sure which Mac mini you have or want to find out about other models, please refer to the Apple support article "Identify the Mac mini model."

Your Mac mini is equipped with advanced technology.

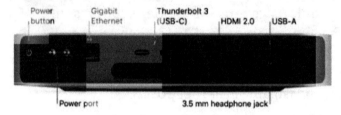

- Power button: Press to open the Mac mini. (Select the "Apple" menu> "Shut down" to turn off the Mac mini, or the "Apple" menu> "Sleep" to make it sleep.)
- Power port: Connect the power cord to the power port on the back of the Mac mini, and then connect the other end of the power cord to the power store.
- Gigabit Ethernet port: Attach a router or modem to use the Internet, or bond to another computer to transfer files without using Wi-Fi.
- 10 Gb Ethernet port (RJ-45): If the Mac mini has a 10 Gb Ethernet port to choose from, you can use N base-T Ethernet technology, which supports high data rates and compares to standard twisted copper cables. up to 10 Gb / s, cable length up to 100 meters (328 meters). Depending on the connected device, the type and technology of the cable used, and the length of the cable, the maximum connection speed is automatically negotiated. For example, if the device you want to connect supports 10 Gbit / s speed, and the cable can sup-

port that speed, both devices will negotiate 10 Gbit / s speeds.

- Thunderbolt 3 (USB-C): Transfer data at Thunderbolt speeds (up to 40 Gbps) and connect to monitors, docking stations, and RAID settings. These ports can charge devices such as iPads or complementary trackpads or keyboards. The Mac mini with the Apple M1 chip has two holes, these ports also support USB 4. Some models have four holes and do not support USB 4.
- HDMI 2.0 port: Use an HDMI adapter to DVI or HDMI cable (sold separately) to connect a Mac mini to a TV or an external monitor. See Connect connector to Mac mini
- USB-A port: connect an iPad, iPhone, iPod, digital camera, external storage device, or printer. The Mac mini USB-A port supports USB 3 and USB 2 devices.
- 3.5 mm jack phone: connect stereo headphones or speakers to hear high-quality audio while listening to music or watching movies. Or connect an analog headset with a built-in monaural microphone for audio and video calls.

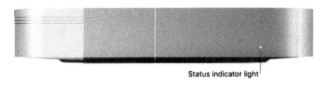

Status indicator light

- Status light: When the indicator light is turned on, it indicates whether the Mac mini is asleep or asleep; when the indicator light is off, it indicates that the Mac mini is off.

Connect accessories to Mac mini

Connect a compatible keyboard, mouse, fingerprint clip, or other optional devices to start using the Mac mini. If you are setting up your Mac mini for the first time, and you need to connect the monitor (for details, see Connect the monitor to your Mac mini).

You can use Bluetooth® technology for wireless work. Your Mac mini can be connected to wireless devices, such as Magic Keyboard, Magic Mouse 2, Magic Trackpad 2, mobile and sports accessories. To connect your Mac mini with your device, in "System Preferences", click on "Bluetooth."

Accessories are sold separately at apple.com, your Apple store, or other retailers.

Use the adapter on the Mac mini

The following Apple adapters can be used to connect external devices, displays, etc. Port of Thunderbolt 3 (USB-C) on Mac mini.

Thunderbolt 3 (USB-C) in Thunderbolt 2 adapter: connect Mac mini to Thunderbolt 2 device or Thunderbolt display.

USB-C digital AV adapter with multiple ports: connect Mac mini to HDMI device, while reconnecting standard USB device.

USB-C VGA adapter for multiple

ports: connect a Mac mini to
a VGA projector or

monitor, while connecting
standard USB

devices.

Learn more. See the Apple Thunderbolt 3 adapter support article or USB-C port on Mac.

Adapters and other accessories are sold separately. Please visit Apple.com, your local Apple Store, or other retailers for more information and availability. Check the documentation or contact the manufacturer to make sure you have selected the appropriate adapter for your Mac mini.

Connect the monitor to the Mac mini

The Thunderbolt 3 (USB-C) port Thunderbolt icon and HDMI 2.0 port both support video output, so you can connect an external monitor, projector, or HDTV.

- On a Mac mini with an Apple M1 chip, you can use the Thunderbolt 3 (USB-C) port to connect an external display up to 6K, and then use the HDMI 2.0 port to connect an external display up to 4K.
- On some Mac mini models, the Thunderbolt 3 (USB-C) port on the Mac mini is controlled by two controllers — one for two ports on the left and one for two ports on the right. You can use Thunderbolt 3 (USB-C) port to connect a 5K monitor, or use two Thunderbolt 3 (USB-C) ports and HDMI 2.0 ports to connect up to three 4K

monitors.

Connect this device to Mac mini	Use cables or adapters and cables
Apple Pro Display XDR (Only Mac mini with Apple M1 chip)	Thunderbolt 3 Cable (USB-C)
Thunderbolt 3 (USB-C) display	Thunderbolt 3 Cable (USB-C)
USB-C display	USB-C cable (USB 3.1)
HDMI or HDTV display	The HDMI cable is provided with a
monitor or HDTV	
Thunderbolt 2 indicator	Thunderbolt 2 (USB-C) to Thun-
derbolt 2 adapter with	the
cable that comes with	Thun-
derbolt 2 monitor	
VGA monitoring or projector adapter	USB-C VGA multiport
	and cable
that comes with a	monitor
or projector	
Display Port Display or	USB-C to Display Port or Mini
Day Display Port	Display Port adapter with cable

that

comes with the monitor

DVI or project monitor   USB-C to DVI adapter with
cable

                                                          monitor

or projector

Adapters and other accessories are sold separately. Please visit Apple.com, your local Apple Store, or other retailers for more information and availability. Check the label or contact the manufacturer to make sure you select the right product. See Thunderbolt 3 adapter or USB-C port on Mac or iPad Pro.

Learn more. For more information on display preferences, please see the Apple Support article Using an external monitor on a Mac. To resolve problems with external monitors, see Getting Help with Video Problems from an external monitor connected to your Mac.

Features of the Mac mini

make-up

With the 2020 M1 update, Apple did not change the design of the Mac mini, but also added silver color. All versions of the M1 Mac mini are silver, while the Intel models are gray in space, and color is the difference between the two.

The Mac mini has always been Apple's smallest and portable desktop, and it hasn't changed. The Mac mini continues to have a small square case 7.7 inches on each side and 1.4 inches in diameter.

The Mac's Apple mini weighs 2.9 pounds, so it's small enough to be placed anywhere you want, and connect the available and display errors. Unlike other Apple computers, the Mac mini does not have a monitor, keyboard, or mouse, so it is a great option for those who want to provide their services.

The Mac mini has several ports on one side and an LED indicator on the other side to let you know its status. There is an Apple symbol on the top of the device. Except for the Apple logo and port label, there are no other marks on the visible part of the machine.

While the emergence of the Mac mini has not changed a few generations ago, Apple redesigned its interior in 2018 to add a new heat dissipation structure to accommodate 8th-power generation chips and all-flash storage. Compared to the Mac mini models before 2018, it has a larger interior, double airflow, and extended ventilation holes, all of which can hold M1 chips.

the harbor

Apple has installed the Mac mini with multiple ports for use with multiple connecting devices at the same time. The M1 Mac mini has two Thunderbolt 3 / USB-C 4 ports on the back of the device. These ports can support USB-C accessories and displays, as well as an HDMI 2.0 port, a Gigabit Ethernet port, and a 3.5 mm main headphone jack. Two USB-A ports and a power cord connection.

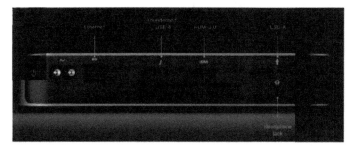

The Intel Mac mini has four Thunderbolt 3 ports, two USB-A ports, a 3.5 mm headphone jack, a power cord socket, and a Gigabit Ethernet port, which can be upgraded to 10Gb. 10Gb Ethernet port updates are limited to the Intel version for Mac mini, not the M1 version.

Thunderbolt 3 provides data transfer speeds up to 40Gb / s. The M1 Mac mini officially supports up to 6K external monitor and an external HDMI monitor up to 4K. The Intel Mac mini is equipped with two 4K displays (and a third 4K display with HDMI) or 5K.

Although Apple claims that the Mac mini is limited to one 6K and 4K display, it has a DisplayPort adapter, while the M1 Mac mini model can run on six external displays. This only applies to the combination of 4K and 1080p displays, because the Thunderbolt port does not have a starting bandwidth of six 4K displays.

M1 Apple Silicon Chip

M1

The 2020 Mac mini is the first Mac collection to be upgraded with an Arm-based chip designed for Apple instead of the Intel chip as the previous Mac mini model. These chips are called "Apple Silicon", and the chip used on the new Mac mini is the M1.

The M1 is the first chip system designed for Apple for Mac, which means it has a processor, GPU, O / O, and security. Tasks and RAM are all integrated into a chip built into the Mac. Apple said this could provide better performance and energy efficiency, thus increasing battery life.

Like Apple's latest A14 chip, the M1 is made using a 5-nanometer processor, making it smaller and more efficient than Apple's predecessors. It has 16 billion transistors, and Apple claims this is the largest transistor invested in a single chip.

Integrated memory construction

One of the M1's functions is integrated memory, UMA, which includes bandwidth, low latency memory. This means that the technology on the M1 chip can access the same data without copying between multiple memory pools, which can greatly improve the performance of the entire system.

The Mac mini supports up to 16GB of integrated memory, and the basic model comes with 8GB.

Speed development

The M1 on the Mac mini has an 8-core CPU and an 8-core GPU integrated. The CPU has four very efficient characters and four cores of high performance. When performing simple tasks such as browsing the Web or reading emails, the Mac mini will use a very efficient core, but for system-enhancing functions such as photo and video editing, it will work for the core functionality.

According to Apple, the CPU speed of the M1 chip is three times that of the Intel chip on the previous Mac mini, while the GPU speed is seven times higher.

If it's cheating combined with notebook chips, the M1 is designed to provide high performance in all electrical power. Compared to the latest PC notebook chips, its CPU performance has increased by 2 times, while power consumption has been reduced by 25%.

Using the M1 chip, ProRes transcoding speed can be increased by up to 3.4 times, the speed of Xcode construction projects can be increased up to 3 times, and Amp Designer plug-in supported by Logic Pro can increase 2.8 times.

Ratings

In the Geekbench bench position test, the M1 chip on the Mac mini has a frequency of 3.2GHz, with more than 1700 single-core points, and a maximum limit of more than 1700. About 7600 points, which makes it faster than the Intel version of the Mac mini Apple still sells.

Besides, the M1 chip on the Mac mini, MacBook Pro, and MacBook Air offers better single-core performance than any other Mac available.

Even if you mimic the x86 under Rosetta 2, the M1 Mac is still faster than all the Macs released earlier. Operating on Apple's Rosetta 2 conversion platform with Geekbench, the Mac can achieve up to 78% to 79% of Apple Silicon code performance.

The benchmark test of the R23 Cinebench chip for the M1 is 7508 (multi-core) and 1498 (single-core). The size of the MacBook Pro, but the Mac mini has the same chip inside.

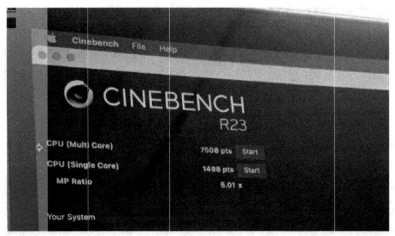

In contrast, the 2020 high-end 16-inch 16-inch MacBook Pro with a 2.3GHz Core i9 chip will get 8818 on multi-core. The low-end 16-inch MacBook Pro 2.6GHz has points -1113, while 69-core multi-core points in the same test were 6912, the previous generation of high-end MacBook Air got 1119 with one core and 4329 with multi-core.

GPU

The 8-core GPU on the M1 chip is integrated (meaning it's not an independent chip), and Apple calls it the world's most integrated graphics on your computers. It can extract 25,000 threads at a time and combine improved graphics performance with lower power consumption.

According to Apple, the GPU on the M1 can provide a timeline up to six times faster than Final Cut Pro, while editing high-resolution images using Affinity Photo can be up to 4 times faster.

In the GFX Bench 5.0 bench test, the M1 beat the GTX 1050 Ti and Radeon RX 560 with a 2.6 TFLOP output.

GPU	Manhattan	T-Rex	ALU 2	Driver Overhead 2	Texturing
Apple M1	407.7 FPS	660.1 FPS	298.1 FPS	245.2 FPS	71,149 MTexels/s
GeForce GTX 1050 Ti	288.3 FPS	508.1 FPS	512.6 FPS	218.2 FPS	59,293 MTexels/s
Radeon RX 560	221.0 FPS	482.9 FPS	6275.4 FPS	95.5 FPS	22,8901 MTexels/s

Neural Engine

There is a new, highly developed engine in the Mac mini that can increase the speed of machine learning tasks 15 times. The neural engine uses a 16-core structure that can make up to 11 billion operations per second, and in combination with a machine learning accelerator, can speed up ML-based operations.

Neural Engines can benefit programs such as Final Cut Pro, Pixelmator, and other programs that use video, image, and audio editing.

Active application

The M1 chip is based on the Arm architecture instead of the x86 build as an Intel chip, but thanks to Rosetta 2 (a back-end and invisible user-rendering process), it can still run applications designed for Intel devices.

Apple also encourages developers to build standard applications that use a single binary file and run on Apple Silicon Macs and Intel Macs. Also, Apple Silicon Macs can launch apps designed for the iPhone and iPad.

We provide detailed information about updated apps with traditional or universal help, games on M1 Mac, customization programs, etc. See our M1 tidbits guide for details.

Intel Mac mini

Apple will continue to sell the Intel Mac mini for new Mac mini models. The Intel Mac mini is equipped with the 8th generation 6-core 3GHz Intel Core i5 chip, which can be upgraded to the Core i7 chip.

The Intel Mac mini is not as fast as the Apple Silicon Mac mini, so it may not be worth buying on the M1 model. Apple may release high-end Mac mini models with Apple silicon chips in the future.

RAM

The basic M1 model is equipped with 8GB RAM, up to 16GB can be customized. Intel high-end models support up to 64GB of RAM. Experiments have shown that there is no significant difference between the M1 model with 8GB RAM and 16GB RAM, except that a large number of system-reinforcing functions are performed.

SSD

The Mac mini supports up to 2TB of solid storage and reads speeds of up to 3.4GB / s.

Connectivity

The M1 Mac mini supports 802.11ax WiFi or WiFi 6, which offers better performance than the previous generation 802.11ac Wi-Fi. Provides 1.2Gb / s throughput for fast file transfer.

The Intel Mac mini supports 802.11ac Wi-Fi, and both models have Bluetooth 5.0.

Get started

How to set up a new Mac mini

If you are just starting to use the Mac mini, don't worry. We are here to help you.

Did you buy your first Mac mini? Want to know how this thing works? This is easier than you think. Like a standalone computer, you can bring your monitor and your mouse to it. The setup method is as follows.

- what do you need
- Set up hardware
- Software setup

what do you need

The new Mac mini is a computer version of Apple barebones. The entry model starts at $ 799 and comes with a Mac mini, power cord, and text. You need to provide your watch eye, keyboard, mouse, or trackpad. Since the new Mac mini has multiple I / O ports, you can choose to display the connection via Thunderbolt 3 connector or HDMI connector. Whether you're using a 5K Thunderbolt display or a 1080p side TV with HDMI, the new Mac mini will be a good choice. The new Mac mini has two USB 3.1 ports, so if you use an old keyboard or mouse, everything will be set up as well.

Set up hardware

1. Make sure your desk or desk can use two power plugs, one for monitoring and one for the new Mac mini. Connect

2. Connect the monitoring cable to the new Mac mini.

3. If you have a new Apple wireless keyboard and trackpad,

you need to connect it with Lightning to a USB cable so that they can both charge and pair with the new Mac mini via Bluetooth. It can be removed after pairing and charging are complete.

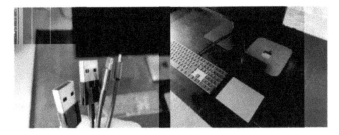

4. After making sure all cables are properly connected, you can press the power button. You will know that the power of the new Mac mini is illuminated with a silver LED on the front.

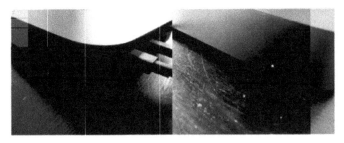

Software setup

1. After booting, a welcome screen will appear.
2. Select your country.
3. Click Continue.
4. Choose your keyboard.
5. Click Continue.

6. Choose your Wi-Fi router and enter a password.
7. Click Continue.
8. (Optional) Read details about Apple's data usage and privacy.
9. Click Continue.

10. Decide if you want to transfer data from backup.
11. Click Continue.
12. (Optional) Sign in with your Apple ID.
13. Click Continue.

14. (Optional) Read the terms and conditions of Apple.
15. Click Continue.
16. If you skipped sign-in with your Apple ID, you now need to create a computer account with a username and password.
17. Click Continue.

18.   You can allow Apple to automatically set various functions, such as Siri and local apps, or you can choose to customize the settings.

19. Click Continue. This process will be completed in a few minutes.

Apple account on Mac

Apple ID is a version that permits you to access all Apple services. Use your Apple ID to download apps from the App Store; access media in Apple Music, Apple Podcast, Apple TV, and Apple Books; use iCloud to keep content up to date on all devices; set up a family sharing group; and More.

You can also use your Apple ID to access other apps and websites (see "Log in with Apple on Mac" in the macOS User Guide).

Important Note: If you forget your Apple ID password, you do not need to create a new Apple ID. Just click the "Forgot Apple ID or password?" In the login window to retrieve your password.

If other family members use Apple devices, make sure each family member has their own Apple ID. You can create your child's Apple ID account and share purchases and subscriptions with "Family Sharing", which will be explained later in this section.

To view available Apple ID services, please check Where I can use Apple ID.

All in one place. Manage everything related to your Apple ID in one place. Open System Favorites on your Mac mini-Apple ID and home-sharing settings are on top.

Apple ID window in system preferences. Click the items in the sidebar to update your account information, open or close iCloud, manage media accounts, and view all devices signed in with Apple ID

Update account, security, and payment details. In "System Preferences", click on "Apple ID" and select an item in the sidebar to view and update the details associated with your account.

- Overview: The "View All" window lets you know that your account is set up and running; if not, you will see tips and notifications here.
- Name, Phone, Email: Update the name and contact details associated with your Apple ID. You can also manage Apple email subscriptions.
- Password and security: Change your Apple ID password, turn on two-factor authentication, add or remove trusted phone numbers, and create a login verification code on another device or iCloud.com. You can also control which programs and websites use "Login with Apple". See "Log in with Apple" in the macOS operator guide.
- Payment and Delivery: Manage payment methods associated with your Apple ID and shipping address from the Apple Store.
- ICloud: Check the checkbox next to the iCloud feature to enable the feature. After enabling the iCloud feature, your content will be stored in iCloud instead of on your Mac, so you can access it on any device that opens iCloud and logs in with the same Apple ID.
- Media and Purchases: Manage accounts associated with Apple Music, Apple Podcast, Apple TV, and Apple Books; select purchase settings; and manage your subscription.

View all your devices. Under the Apple ID sidebar, view all devices connected to Apple ID. You can check if "Find My Device" is open on each device (see "Find My Device"), check the Cloud

Backup status for iOS or iPadOS devices, or if you are no longer the owner of the device, start to Remove Device from on account.

Family sharing. By sharing families, you can set up family groups and create Apple ID accounts for your children. To manage your family sharing settings, click on "Family Sharing" in "System Preferences" and select the icon in the sidebar to view and update your details. You can add or remove family members; share media purchases, payment methods, iCloud storage, and location; and set your children's screen time limits (see Screen Time on Mac).

Find your way around

Desktop, menu bar, and help on Mac

The first thing you see on a Mac mini is a desktop, where you can quickly open programs, search anything on the Mac mini and the Web, edit files, and more.

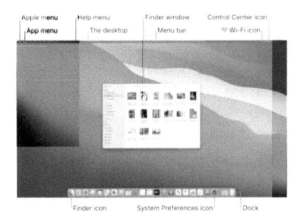

Tip: Can't find the screen on the screen? To zoom in a moment, quickly slide the mouse back and forth.

Menu bar. The menu bar works at the top of the screen. Use the left-hand menu to select commands and perform tasks in the application. The menu items will change depending on the application you are using. Use the icon on the right to connect to the Wi-Fi network, check the Wi-Fi status and the Wi-Fi status icon, open the "Control Center", "Control Center" icons, use the Spotlight icon, Spotlight search, etc. always.

Tip: You can change the icon displayed in the menu bar. See Control Center on Mac.

Apple Menu. Apple's menu contains frequently used commands and is always displayed in the upper left corner of the screen. To open it, click the Apple icon.

Application menu. You can open multiple applications and windows at once. The name of the active application will be displayed in bold on the right side of the Apple menu, and then the only menu for that application. When you open another application or click an open window in another application, the name of the application menu will change to that application, and the menu item will also change accordingly. If you are looking for a command in the menu and can't find the command, check the system menu to see if the system you want is working.

Help menu. Mac mini help is always provided in the menu bar. For help, open the Portal Finder, click the "Help" menu, then select "MacOS Help" to open the macOS User Guide. Or type in the search field and select suggestions. For specific app help, open the app and click "Help" in the menu bar.

For more information, please refer to the macOS User Guide.

Stay organized with stacking. You can use desktops on a desktop to organize files into groups (by category, date, or label) and keep the desktop clean. To view stack content, click the stack to expand its content, or place the cursor on the stack to view file icons. To create a stack on the desktop, click on desktop and select View> Use Stack or press Control-Command-0. You can also hold the Control key and click on the desktop, then select "Use Stack". To view stack collection options, go to View> Group By, and select an option. After that, all new files you add to the desktop are automatically sorted into the appropriate stack. To learn more, see Organizing files in the file stack on Mac in the macOS User Guide.

Read on to find out about Finder and other desktop features on your Mac.

Finder on Mac

Use Finder to organize and retrieve files. To open the Finder window, click the Finder icon in the Dock at the bottom of the screen.

Sync devices. When you connect a device such as an iPhone or iPad, you can see it in the Finder sidebar. From there you can backup, update and restore the device.

Gallery views. Using "Gallery View", you can see the preview of the selected file, so you can view photos, video clips, and other documents. The preview window displays details to help you identify the file you need. Use the wash bar at the bottom to quickly find what you need. To close or open the preview window, press Shift-Command-P.

Tip: To display the file name in "Gallery View", press Command-J and select "Show Name File".

Scrubber bar   Combine PDFs, trim audio and
video files, and automate tasks.

Take immediate action. In the lower right corner of the "Preview" shortcut window lets you manage and edit files directly in the Finder. You can rotate an image into a caption, define or cut an image, merge an image and a PDF into a single file, cut audio and video files, or create a custom action (for example, watermark files) with Automator workflow.

To show Preview options in Finder, select View> Show Preview. To customize the displayed content, select View> Preview Options, and then select your file type options. See Perform quick actions on Finder on Mac in macOS User Guide.

Tip: choose a file and press the space bar to open "Speedly Get". You can sign the PDF; cut audio and video files; then mark, rotate, and crop the images without opening a separate program. To learn more about quick access and tagging tasks, see Use Quick Find on Mac to view and edit files and mark files on Mac in the macOS User Guide.

Dock on Mac

The Dock at the bottom of the screen is an easy place to store apps and documents that you often use.

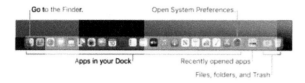

Open the program or file. Click the app icon in Dock, or click the launchpad icon in Dock to view all the apps on your Mac, and then click the app you want. You can also use Spotlight (in the upper right corner of the menu bar) to search for an app, and then open the app directly from Spotlight search results. Recently opened applications will be displayed in the middle section of the Dock.

Close the app. When you click the red dot in the upper left corner of the open window, the window closes, but the app stays open. In Dock, there is a black dot under the open app. To close the application, select "Exit in Application Name" from the application menu (for example, in the "Email" application, select "Exit Email" from the "Email" menu). Or press the Control key and click the Application icon in Dock, then click "Exit".

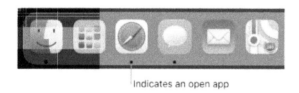

Indicates an open app

Insert the object into Dock. Drag and drop the thing at the chosen location. Install the application on the left side of the Dock, then insert the file or folder into the appropriate section.

Remove item from the port. Drag and drop out Dock. The item will not be removed from the Mac mini, but only from the Dock.

View all open content on your Mac. Press the task control key on the keyboard to view open windows, desktop space, full-screen apps, etc., to easily switch between them. You can also add task control icons to Dock. Please see the Apple Support article Using "Task Control" on Mac.

Tip: Click Dock and the menu preferences menu to change Dock's appearance and behavior. Zoom in or out, drop it to the left or right of the screen, set it to hide when not in use, and so on.

Notification Center on Mac

The notification center has been redesigned to save all important information, reminders, and widgets in a convenient location. Get detailed information on calendar events, stocks, weather, etc., and receive notifications (emails, messages, reminders, etc.) you may have missed.

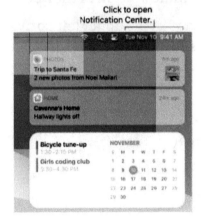

Open the notification center. Click the date or time in the top right corner of the screen, or use two fingers to swipe left from the right edge of the trackpad. Scroll down to see more.

Share your notifications. Reply to emails, listen to recent podcasts, or view detailed information on calendar events. Click the arrow in the top right corner of the notification to view options, take action, or get more information.

Customize your widget. Click Edit Widgets to add, delete or rearrange widgets. You can as well add third-party widgets from the Mac App Store.

Set your notification preferences. Open Method Preferences and click Notices to select which notifications you see. Notifications are updated recently, and the redesigned "Modern" widget makes the details clearer.

Control Center on Mac

The new "Control Center" integrates the entire menu bar in one place, allowing you to instantly access the most commonly used controls, such as Bluetooth, AirDrop, screenshot, and light and volume control, directly from the menu bar. Click the Control Center icon in the top right corner of the screen to open the control center.

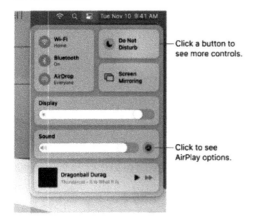

Click for more options. Click the button to see more options. For instance, click the Wi-Fi button to view your preferred network, other networks, or to open "Network Preferences." To return to the main control center view, click the Control Center icon again.

Pin your "Control Center" preferences. Drag your favorite item from the "Control Center" to the menu bar anywhere, so you can easily access it with a single click. To correct the content showed in the Control Center and Menu Bar, open the Dock & Menu Bar Favorites, choose the controller on the left, and then tap"Show in Menu Bar" or "Show in Control Center". You will see the controls will appear in the preview menu. Some items cannot be added or removed from the control center or menu bar.

Tip: To quickly remove an item from the menu bar, grab the Command key and drag it out of the menu.

System Favorites on Mac

System preferences are when you customize your Mac mini settings. For instance, use "Energy Saver" preferences to change sleep settings. Or use the "Desktop and Screen Server" preferences to add a desktop background or select screen saver.

Customize your Mac mini. Select the "Apple" menu> "System Favorites", or tap the "System preference" icon in the Dock. Then click the type of favorite you want to set. To learn more, see "Modify Mac with System Favorites" in the macOS User Guide.

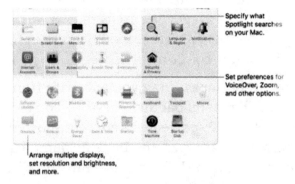

Update macOS. In System Preferences, click Software Update to see if your Mac is using the latest version of macOS software. You can specify automatic software update options.

Focus on Mac

The Spotlight Spotlight icon is an easy way to find anything on the Mac mini, such as documents, contacts, calendar events, and emails. Exposure suggestions provide information from Wikipedia articles, web search results, news, sports, weather, stocks, movies, and other sources.

Search for anything. Click the Spotlight icon at the top right of the screen and start typing.

Tip: Type Command-Spacebar to show or hide the Spotlight search field.

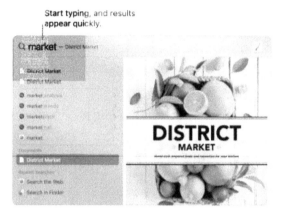

Change currencies and metrics. Enter the amount (for example, $, € or ¥) with the amount, and press the Return key to get a list of converted prices. Or specify a unit of measurement conversion.

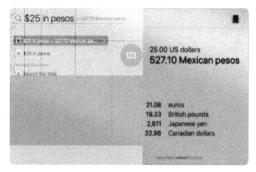

Open the app. Enter the app name in Spotlight and press Return.

Turn off Spotlight suggestions. If you want to highlight search items on Mac mini only, open "System Preferences", click "Spotlight", and then click "Siri Suggestions" You can also make some changes to the list of visual search categories.

Siri on Mac

You can talk to Siri on your Mac mini and use voice to perform many tasks. For example, you can find files, schedule meetings, change preferences, get feedback, send messages, make calls, and add items to the calendar. Siri can give you directives ("How do I get home from here?"), Give you fine points ("How high is Mount Whitney?"), Perform complex tasks ("form a new menu"), and more.

Note: To use Siri, your Mac must be connected to the Internet. Siri may not be vacant in all languages or regions, and features could vary by region.

Important Note: The Mac mini does not have a built-in microphone, so you must connect an external microphone (sold separately) to use Siri. After connecting the microphone, select "Sound" preferences (open "System Preferences", click "Sound", click "Input", and select your microphone).

Enable Siri. Open System Preferences, click Siri and set options. If Siri is enabled during the setup process, press and hold Command-Spacebar to unlock Siri. Or click Siri on the system preferences, and select Allow to ask Siri. You can also set other options, such as the language and voice used, and that you can show Siri in the menu bar.

Talk to Siri. Hold the Command-Spacebar and start talking. By selecting this option in the Siri window of the system preferences, the Siri icon can be added to the menu bar. Then click the Siri icon to apply Siri.

Tip: To learn more about using Siri, please feel free to ask "What you can do" or click the "Help" button.

Play music. Just say "play music" and Siri does something else. You can say Siri: "Play rare songs from old days."

Find and open the file. Let Siri find the files and open them directly from the Siri window. You can ask by file name or description. For example, "Show files I sent to Ursula" or "Open spreadsheet I created last night."

Drag and drop. Drag and drop a photo and a location from the Siri window into an email, text message, or document. You can copy and paste the text.

Change the voice. Click Siri on the system preferences, then selects an option from the Siri voice menu.

Display Settings for your Mac

Use a powerful desktop. If you use a powerful desktop image, the desktop image will automatically change to match the time of day in your area. In "System Favorites", click on "Desktop and Screen Saver", then click on "Desktop", then select the "Dynamic Desktop" image. To change the screen depending on the time zone, please enable location services. When "Location Tasks" is turned off, the image will change according to the time zone specified in the "Date and Time" preferences.

Use the black mode to stay focused. You can use the black desktop scheme, menu bar, Dock, and all built-in MacOS apps. Your content is highlighted in the front and the middle, while the dim controls and windows are back. You see white text in dark background in apps such as "Email", "Contacts", "Calendar" and "Messages", so your vision will be easier when working in a dark place.

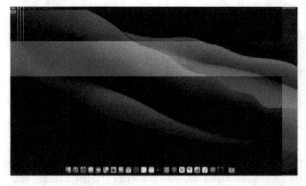

The dark mode is for professionals who edit photos and images - colors and fine details will appear in the background of the black app. Also great for those who just want to focus on their content.

Use the Mac mini as a server

The most popular file servers, time server, and cache server - are part of macOS, so the Mac mini can be easily used as a server. Open System Preferences and click Share to access one or more of the options below.

- File Server: Use file sharing to allow users to save and share folders and files on Mac mini. See Set file sharing on Mac in macOS user directory.
- Time server: Use file sharing to allow users to use file sharing to back up their Mac computers to Mac mini. Please refer to Time Machine on Mac to back up the shared folder in the macOS User Guide.
- Cache Server: Use the Content Manager to provide a temporary repository of software distributed by Apple over the Internet.

Transfer data to a new Mac mini

It's easy to move files and settings from one Mac or PC to a Mac mini. You can transfer data on a Mac mini from Time Machine backup to an old computer or device via a wireless or Ethernet cable and adapter.

You may need to upgrade the MacOS version to your old computer before transferring data. Migration Assistant needs MacOS 10.7 or higher, but it's best to upgrade an old computer to the latest version. If you're not sure which Mac mini you have or want to find out about other models, please refer to the Apple support article "Identify the Mac mini model."

Tip: For best results, make sure the new Mac mini uses the latest version of macOS. Open System Preferences and click Software Update to check for updates.

Move from PC to Mac. If you are a new Mac user and want to transfer from a Windows computer, please refer to the macOS user guide for transferring data from PC to Mac, and the Apple support article Transferring your data from Windows PC to Mac.

Wireless transmission. To transfer data when you set up a Mac mini for the first time, use Setup Assistant. To transfer data over time, use the Migration Assistant. Open the Finder window, go to "Applications", open "Applications", and double-click "Migration Assistant" to make wireless migration. Follow the instructions on the screen. Make sure both computers are connected to the same network and keep both computers close to each other during the migration process.

Tip: Quick migration, use a cable (such as a Thunderbolt 3 (USB-C) cable) to connect an old computer to a Mac mini.

If you use Time Machine to back up files from another Mac to storage (such as an external disk), you can copy files from that device to a Mac mini. See Back up and Restore the Mac.

Copy files from storage devices. Connect the storage device to the USB-A port, USB icon, or Thunderbolt 3 (USB-C) port or Thunderbolt icon to the Mac mini, and then drag the file from the storage device to the Mac mini.

Restore your content. To learn how to restore a Mac from Time Machine or other backups, see the Apple support article Restore Mac for backup.

Back up and restore the Mac

To ensure file security, it is very important to back up your Mac mini regularly. An easy way to backup is to backup your apps, accounts, preferences, music, photos, movies, and texts using Time Machine built into your Mac (doesn't back up the macOS app). Use Time Machine to backup to an external storage device connected to a Mac mini or supported network volume. For a list of Time Machine supported devices, please refer to the Apple Backup Disk Support Article that can be used with Time Machine.

Tip: You can use the Mac shared on the same network as the Mac mini as your storage location. On another Mac, go to the "Share" "Preferences System" panel and open "File Sharing". To add a shared folder, hold Control and click the folder, select "Advanced Options", then click "Share as Time Machine Backup Destination".

Set the timer. Make sure the Mac mini and external storage device are on the same Wi-Fi network or connect the storage device to the Mac mini. Open "System Preferences", click on "Machine Time", and select "Auto Backup". Select the drive you want to use for backup, and everything is ready.

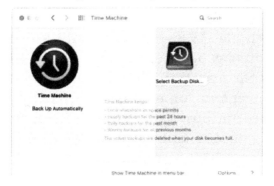

Files in iCloud Drive and photos in iCloud Photos are automatically saved to iCloud and do not need to be part of a backup. However, if you want to back up, do the following:

- iCloud Drive: Open "System Favorites", click "Apple ID", then click "iCloud" and uncheck "Optimize Mac Storage". Cloud Drive content will be stored on Mac and backed up.
- iCloud Photos: Open Photos, and select Photos> Preferences. In the "iCloud" window, select "Real Download

on this Mac." The full version of the image library optimization will be stored on Mac and backed up.

Restore files. You can use Time Machine to retrieve all files at once. Click the Time Machine icon in the menu bar and select Insert Machine Time. (If there is no "Time Machine" icon in the menu bar, select "Apple Menu"> "System Favorites", click "Time Machine", and then select "Show Time Machine in the menu bar".) Select one or more items to be restored (one folder or all disk), and then click "Restore".

If you use Time Machine to back up your Mac, you can restore files if an application or boot disk is damaged. To do this, you must install macOS on your Mac before using Time Machine backups to recover files. Read on for more details.

Reinstall macOS. Active system files and personal files are stored on a separate system disk. However, some tasks (such as wiping or accidentally damaging a disk) require you to restore your Mac mini. You can reinstall macOS and use Time Machine to restore your files from backup. With macOS Big Sur, there are several ways to restore your Mac. You may be asked to install the latest version of macOS instead of the macOS version that comes first with your computer, or the version you used before disk damage. To learn more about these options, see "Restore all files from Time Machine backup" in the macOS user guide and Apple support article "How to reinstall macOS in macOS recovery."

Important: Advanced users may want to create a bootable installer to install macOS in the future. This is useful if you want to use some form of macOS. See the Apple support article How to create a stumbling block for macOS.

Availability on Mac

Your Mac, iOS, and iPadOS device include powerful tools that make Apple product features accessible and easy for everyone to use. Mac has four access points to focus on. Click the link to learn more about the features of each location:

- Just think
- Hearing
- Liquid
- Read

For more information on Apple's accessibility support, please visit Availability.

Accessibility preferences. In the "System Preferences" preferences, "Accessibility" is now set to visual, audio and sports themes, making it easy to find what you need.

Use voice control to complete all tasks. You can only control your Mac with audio. All voice processing voice control is done on the device, so your data will be kept private.

Important note: The Mac mini does not have a built-in microphone, so you must connect an external microphone (sold separately) to use voice control.

Accurate call. If you cannot enter text by hand, accurate pronunciation is essential for communication. Voice control brings the latest advances in machine learning from speech to text.

You can add custom words to help control the voice to see your frequently used words. Select "System Preferences"> "Accessibility", select "Voice Control", then click "Vocabulary" and enter the words you want. To customize the commands on the Voice Control Preferences page, click Commands and choose to save the default commands or add new commands.

Note: Improved pronunciation accuracy only applies to American English.

Editing rich text. RTF editing commands in voice control allow you to make quick adjustments and then proceed to express your next thought. You can change one phrase to another, quickly set the cursor to edit, and select the text correctly. Try "John has just arrived" instead of "John will be coming soon.". When correcting words, word suggestions and emojis can help you quickly choose what you need.

Perfect navigation. Use voice commands to open and interact with applications. To click on an item, simply specify its accessibility label name. You can also say "show numbers" to show the number label next to each clickable item, then say the number you want to click. If you need to touch the part of the screen without controls, you can say "show grid" to hover the grid on the screen and perform tasks such as clicking, zooming in, dragging, etc.

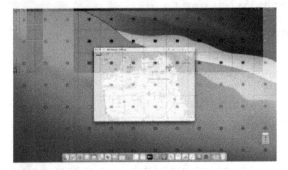

Move up and zoom in. Use the navigation text to display the text's high definition text below the cursor. When you hover your mouse over the text, press the Command button, and a window with enlarged text appears on the screen.

The zoom indicator allows you to zoom in on one monitor, while the other maintains its standard resolution. Watch the same screen closer or closer.

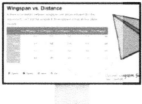

Use VoiceOver Secret. If you like Siri's natural sound, you can choose to use VoiceOver Siri or Speech Siri. Simplified keyboard navigation requires less drilling in a separate focus group, making it easier to navigate with VoiceOver. You can also save custom typing icons on the Cloud and select from the international braille table. Also, if you are an engineer, VoiceOver can now read line numbers, breakpoints, alerts, and errors in the Xcode text editor.

Color enhancement. If you do not see the color correctly, you can use the new color filtering options to adjust the display colors of your Mac. Use the "Accessibility Options" panel to turn on or off your preferences to quickly distinguish colors, and you can access this panel by pressing Command-Option-F5.

New features for Mac mini

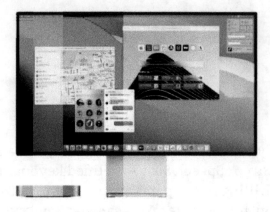

The Mac mini with the Apple M1 chip has powerful functionality, graphics, and other technological improvements to run your preferred apps faster than previously. The most notable changes are the support for USB 4 devices and the ability to connect to external 6K displays (such as the Apple Pro Display XDR).

macOS Big Sur introduces a new look for the Mac desktop, designed to integrate Apple devices. The new design includes a flexible base and menu, updated but custom icons, and a wide menu. The full height sidebar and the integrated toolbar buttons make the app easy to use. Even the sound you hear when you receive a notification or warning has been updated.

The new design makes navigation easier and gives you more control over the following features:

- **Control Center:** The new control center puts all your favorite menu items in one place, so you can quickly access controls and most popular preferences (such as Wi-Fi, AirDrop, and Bluetooth). See Control Center on Mac.
- **Notification Center:** A redesigned notification center shows your notifications and widgets in one column. You can customize the widgets you see and share notifications (for example, reply to emails). The "weather" widget is accurate and warns of bad weather or major changes. Please check the notification center on your Mac.

In addition to the redesign, MacOS Big Sur has also significantly improved on these important applications:

- **Safari:** Since Safari was first released in 2003, it is the largest update to Safari, providing an instant browsing experience. Make your browsing experience richer with the new customizable homepage, and get many more extensions in the App Store. Use the brand new Favicon on the label and the label preview from there to scroll up for easy browsing. Click the translation icon to quickly translate web pages (beta) into 7 supported languages. Safari also provides a new privacy report showing how you are protecting your privacy on various websites you are browsing. Safari has become the world's fastest desktop browser. Compared to Chrome or Firefox, it offers faster-browsing speed and longer battery life. See Safari.
- **Maps:** The newly selected guides can help you find the best places to eat, shop, and visit, and you can make your guides. Use "View Around" to take parallel 3D tours of selected city streets. You can now set up a bike path that gives you directions to altitudes and obstacles, or an electric bike route, with charging stops and timing. Indoor maps are ideal for major airports and shopping malls, so you can easily find restaurants, toilets, and shops. See the map.
- **Messaging:** New tools make it easy to share and display messages and manage group chats. With the new message effect, you can customize the message with balloons, confetti, etc. Add Memoji stickers that match your mood and personality to the conversation, and use the Memoji editor on your Mac to create new stickers. You can even instantly share GIFs or best photos in your photo library with # images and a new photo clip. The new group messaging feature makes communication easier with family, friends, and colleagues. Pin

your favorite conversations at the top of the address list for quick access. Reply directly to messages using in-line answers, then send a direct message to someone in the group chat by simply typing their name. Set photos or emojis in group discussions and share them with all group members. See message.

macOS Big Sur also offers the following new features and enhancements to existing features:

- **AirPods:** AirPods can switch seamlessly between active devices connected to the same iCloud account, making it easier to use AirPods and Apple devices. On a Mac, you can click the notification to change the audio from another device. Device switches can be used with AirPods Pro, AirPods (second generation), Powerbeats, Powerbeats Pro, and Beats Solo Pro. Requires an iPhone or iPod with the latest version of iOS; iPad with the latest version of iPadOS; or Mac with the latest version of macOS.
- **Apple Arcade**: See what games your G friends have a stand in the Play Center directly from the Arcade tab, and check out your achievements and objectives on the game page. Game Center now features an in-game dashboard to check your progress with your friends at a glance. Please refer to the App Store.
- **Family Sharing:** An improved user interface for family settings makes family members more transparent and can control their family settings. Setting up a family, adding new members, and managing family details is easier than ever. Learn more about family sharing in "Cloud Content" on Mac and "Apple Account" on Mac.
- **Homepage:** The "Homepage" app has some improvements, including a visual view and a summary of the following: attachments that require attention or sharing of important status, facial recognition and function of gate and camera doors, and familiarity with smart light bulbs. Please refer to the homepage.

- **iPhone and iPad apps on Mac mini with Apple M1 chip**: Now, most iPhone and iPad apps with Apple M1 chip can work on your Mac mini. Please refer to the App Store.
- **Listen Now**: In the "Music and Podcasts", the "Listen Now" tab lets you understand your interests (such as artists, chats, remixes, podcasts) and offers suggestions based on your listening content. The podcast features a more focused Up Next, so you can easily proceed to the next episode online. See music and podcasts.
- **Notes:** The new text style provides you with many note formatting options. Improved scanning functionality on iPhone helps you to capture clear scans and transfer them to your Mac for immediate use. See note.
- **Photos:** Video and photo editing enhanced with filters, special effects, etc. You can refine your refined image and add captions to photos and videos. Memory enhancement includes many music and video enhancement music tracks. See pictures.
- **Reminders**: Separate tasks and get smart suggestions for using reminders in new ways. Give reminders to people who have shared the list with you and they will be notified. You can also let smart suggestions help you create reminders based on the same reminders created in the past. When you contact someone by Mail, Siri will point out potential reminders and give you suggestions for making suggestions. Then use the new keyboard shortcut to quickly find the reminder you need. See reminder.
- **Software Update:** With macOS Big Sur, the software update starts in the background, and the update speed is much faster than before, so it's easy to keep your Mac up to date and secure.
- **Brightness:** Brightness is much faster than before. Now, it will highlight your top search results and suggestions as you type, so you can quickly access high-quality suggestions. Visual technology is also used in the "Discover" apps menu such as Safari, Pages, and Keynote. View

brightness on Mac.

- **Voice memo**: Install folders to help you keep your voice memo organized. Easily mark the recordings as "favorites" so you can access them quickly later. With a single click, background sound can be reduced automatically, thus taking Voice Memos one step further. (External microphone required. Accessories are sold separately at Apple.com, your local Apple Store, or other retailers.) Please refer to the voice memo.

Use Mac mini with other devices

Use Mac mini with iCloud and continue

There are many ways to use a Mac mini with an iPhone, iPad, iPod touch, or Apple Watch. You can transfer files, share and edit documents, use Apple Watch to unlock Mac mini, turn your iPhone or iPad into an Internet hotspot, and so on.

Access your content across devices. With iCloud, you can securely store, organize, and share documents, photos, and videos across devices to ensure they stay up to date. To get started, see Access your iCloud content on Mac.

If you did not turn on iCloud when you set up your Mac for the first time, please open "System Favorites", click "Sign In", and sign in with your Apple ID. If not, please create a new Apple ID. Click iCloud, then open or close the iCloud function. For more information, please refer to Setting iCloud on Mac in the macOS User Guide.

Use Mac mini and other devices. You can use the Continuous switch freely between Mac mini and other devices. Just use your Apple ID to sign in on each device, and whenever the Mac mini and device are close, they can easily interact. You can start work on one device, then complete a task on another device (see "Use Switch" on Mac), copy and paste between devices (see "Use Universal Clipboard" on Mac), answer calls or send messages from Mac mini (see " Phone ") and text messages on Mac), use AirDrop to transfer files (see Use AirDrop on Mac), etc. For more placement details, see the following sections.

For a list of program requirements for Supporting Devices, please refer to the Apple Support Article Process System Requirements for Mac, iPhone, iPad, iPod touch, and Apple Watch. To learn more about Continuity on Mac mini, please refer to the Apple support article "Use Continuity to connect Mac, iPhone, iPad, iPod touch and Apple Watch connection" or go to "All devices ".

Access your iCloud content on a Mac

Cloud is an easy way to ensure that all-important content is accessible everywhere. Cloud stores your documents, photos, music, apps, contacts, and calendars, so you can access them whenever you're connected to a network.

You can use your Apple ID to set up a free iCloud account with 5 GB of free storage. Products you purchase in the iTunes Store, App Store, Apple TV, or Book Store will not be included in your location available.

Cloud keeps everything on your device up to date. So if you have an iPhone, iPad, or iPod touch, just log in to each device with your Apple ID, then open iCloud, and you'll have everything you need.

For system requirements for devices that support iCloud, please refer to the Apple Support Article iCloud Requirements.

Here are some of the functions you can use in the Cloud.

Automatically save your desktop and Documents folder to iCloud Drive. You can save files to a "Documents" folder or your desktop, and they will be automatically found on iCloud Drive and can be found anywhere. If you use iCloud Drive, you can access the files on your Mac mini, the "Files" app on your iPhone or iPad, iCloud.com on the web, or your Windows PC in the iCloud app. When you make changes to a file on your device or iCloud drive, you can see the changes wherever you look.

First, open "System Preferences", click on "Apple ID", then click on "iCloud". Select "Cloud Drive", then click "Options", then select "Desktop Folders and Documents." To learn more, check out Apple's support article "Adding Desktop and Document Files to Cloud Drive".

Share shopping and storage and family sharing. Up to six family members can share items purchased from the App Store, the Apple TV app, the Book Store, and the iTunes Store, and share the same storage plan, even if each of them uses his or her iCloud account. Use a credit card to pay for home purchases and allow your child to use directly from a Mac mini, iOS device, or iPadOS device. You can share photos, family calendars, reminders, and places. If you did not set home sharing when you set up your Mac, open System Preferences, click Home Sharing, and then click Next. To learn more, see the Apple Support article "Set Up Family Sharing."

Use iCloud Photos and Shared Albums to store and share photos. Store photos in iCloud, then view photos and videos and edit them on all devices. Only share photos and videos with the people you choose, and let them add their photos, videos, and comments. First, open "System Favorites", click "Apple ID", then click "iCloud", then select "Photos". To learn more, see the Apple support article "Setting and using iCloud Photos."

Enjoy shopping everywhere. After signing in to a device with the same Apple ID, no matter what computer or device you use, you can always shop in the App Store, Apple TV application, Book Store, and iTunes Store. Buy them. So, wherever you are, you can use all the music, movies, books, etc.

Use "Find My Mac" to find your Mac mini. If your Mac mini is lost, you can use "Find My Mac" to find it on the map with "Find My Mac" open, lock its screen, and erase its data remotely. To open "Find My Mac", open "System Favorites", click "Apple ID", click "iCloud", and then select "Find My Mac". Please refer to the Apple Support article if your Mac is lost or stolen.

Note: If your Mac mini has multiple user accounts, only one can open "Find My Mac".

Screenshot on Mac

Screen time shows how you spend your time on apps and websites. It also allows you to monitor your child's activities on Apple devices.

Set your limits. Set time limits for spending time on specific apps, app categories, and websites. You can also view reports to see how much time you spend on apps and websites and schedule a Mac free time.

Family sharing. Parents can configure "Screen Time" on a Mac or iPhone or iPad, and all settings can be set for their children on the device.

Rate media with one click. When you set your child's "Screen Time", you can set media ratings based on the age of the "Music and Books" app.

Use conversion on Mac

With "handover", you can continue on one device without using it on another. Process the presentation on the Mac mini, then continue on the iPad. Or start an email on iPhone, and complete email on Mac mini. Check the message on the Apple Watch, then reply to the Mac mini. You do not have to worry about transferring files. When the Mac mini and device are close, as long as operations are possible, an icon will appear in the Dock. To continue, simply click on the icon.

Note: To use Handoff, you need an iPhone or iPod touch with iOS 8 or later, or an iPad with iPadOS. Make sure your Mac mini, iOS device, or iPadOS has Wi-Fi and Bluetooth turned on, and sign in with the same Apple ID.

Open "Switch" on Mac mini. Open "System Preferences", click "General", then select "Allow switching between this Mac and iCloud device".

Open "Switch" on your iOS or iPadOS device. Go to "Settings"> "General"> "Change" and tap to open "Change". If you do not see this option, your device does not support switching.

Open "Convert" to Apple Watch. In the Apple Watch app on your iPhone, go to "Settings"> "General" and tap to enable "Allow conversion".

The switch function works in Safari, email, calendar, contacts, maps, messages, notes, reminders, key expressions, numbers, and pages.

Use Universal Clipboard on Mac

Copy content from one device and paste it to another nearby device in a short time. Content on the sticker board is sent via Wi-Fi and can be used on all Mac, iPhone, iPad, and iPod devices that log in with the same Apple ID and are enabled for Handoff, Wi-Fi, and -Bluetooth. See Use handoff on Mac.

Note: To use Universal Clipboard, you need an iPhone or iPod touch with iOS 10 or later, or an iPad with iPadOS.

Apply to all applications. You can copy and paste photos, text, photos, and videos among any apps that support copying and pasting on Mac, iPhone, iPad, and iPod touch.

Copy and paste the files. You can use the universal pasteboard to quickly move files from one Mac to another. Copy the file to the Mac mini and paste it into the Finder window, email message, or any other application on the nearby Mac that supports copy and paste. On both Macs, you must sign in with the same Apple ID.

Sidecar on Mac

With Sidecar, you can turn your iPad into a subsequent display for your Mac. Give yourself more workspace, draw with Apple Pencil, mark PDFs, and screenshots, etc.

Note: You can use Sidecar with iPad models that support Apple Pencil and use iPadOS 13 (or higher). For more information, see the Apple Support Pics link for the Apple Pencil on the iPad and use the iPad as a second display for Mac and Sidecar.

Connect your iPad. Click the "Control Center" icon in the menu bar to open the "Control Center", click "Screen Mirroring", then click "Screen Mirroring", and then select your iPad. After enabling Sidecar, the icon will switch to the blue iPad icon. To disconnect the iPad on Mac, open the AirPlay menu and select Disconnect. You can also disconnect by clicking the "Disconnect" icon in the iPad sidebar.

Tip: If you do not see the iPad in the AirPlay menu, please ensure that the Wi-Fi or Bluetooth function of the iPad is turned on. You also need to sign in with the same Apple ID on both devices.

Wired or wireless. Connect the iPad with a cable and keep it charged, or use the iPad wirelessly within 10 meters of Mac.

Extend your desktop. When you connect an iPad, it will automatically become a desktop extension for Mac. To get started, simply drag your apps and documents to the iPad.

The screen of your desktop. To display the Mac screen on both devices, open the "Screen mirroring" menu and the "Screen mirroring" icon in the "Control Center", then select "Mirror the retina display". To expand the desktop again, open the menu and select "Use as a separate monitor."

Use the Apple Pencil. Directly design and create technology applications of your choice. Just drag the window from Mac to iPad and start using Apple Pencil. Or use Apple Pencil to mark PDFs, screenshots, and photos. To learn more, see Continuity Sketch and Continuity Markup on Mac.

Note: The pressure and inclination of the Apple Pencil are only allowed for applications with advanced pen support.

Use sidebar shortcuts. Use the sidebar on the iPad to quickly access frequently used buttons and controls. Press the button to undo the operation, use the keyboard shortcuts and show or hide the menu bar, Dock, and keyboard.

Use touch bar controls with or without a touch bar. For apps with Touch Bar support, controls will be displayed at the bottom of the iPad display even if your Mac has Touch Bar.

Set preferences. To set Sidecar preferences, open "System Preferences" and click on "Sidecar". Or select "Sidecar Preferences" from the "Screen Mirroring" menu in the Control Center. You can specify the device you want to connect to, change the sidebar and touch the bar on the iPad, and double-tap with the Apple Pencil for quick access to tools.

Camera continuity on Mac

Use an iPhone, iPad, or iPod touch to scan a document or take a close-up photo, and it will instantly appear on your Mac. Many applications support Continuity Camera, including Finder, Email, Messages, etc.

Note: To use the continuous camera, you need an iPhone or iPod touch with iOS 12 (or higher) or an iPad with iPadOS 13 (or higher). Make sure your Mac mini and iOS or iPadOS device has Wi-Fi and Bluetooth turned on, and sign in with the same Apple ID.

Insert an image or scan. For applications such as "Email", "Notes" or "Messages", select the location where you want to move the image, select "File (or insert)"> "Import from iPhone or iPad", select "Take the photo" or Scan Document "and take a photo or scan a photo on your iOS or iPadOS device. Before taking a photo, you may need to select an iOS or iPadOS device. Click Apply Image or continue scanning. If you want to try again, you can also click Restart.

For page-like applications, select the location where you want to insert the image, then hold down the control button and click, select "Import image", and take a picture. Before taking a photo, you may need to select a device.

Note: To scan on an iOS or iPadOS device, drag the frame until the content to be displayed appears in the frame, then click "Save Scan" and "Save" respectively. Click Restart to re-scan the content.

The image or scan appears in the desired location in the document.

Continuation drawings and progression marks on Mac

With continuous drawing, you can use an iPhone or iPad nearby to draw drawings and instantly upload them to documents on your Mac, for example, emails, messages, documents, or notes. Or use "Continuous Symbols" to edit a document with your finger on an iOS device or Apple Pencil on an iPad, and view these tags on a Mac.

Note: To use Continuity Sketch and Continuity Markup, you need an iPhone or iPod touch with iOS 13 (or higher) or an iPad with iPadOS 13 (or higher). Make sure your Mac mini and iOS or iPadOS device has Wi-Fi and Bluetooth turned on, and sign in with the same Apple ID. Apple Pencil Pressure and Tilt only apply to apps with the help of advanced writing.

Insert drawing. For applications such as mail, notes, or messages, place the cursor where you want to insert the drawing. Select "File (or Install)"> "Import from iPhone or iPad", then select "Install Sketch". On an iOS or iPad device, use your finger or the Apple Pencil (on the iPad supporting the iPad) to draw a drawing, then click on "Finish". On a Mac, a drawing appears where the cursor is located. Depending on where you place the drawing, you can mark it or adjust other features, such as enlargement.

Mark the text. For continuous tagging, you can use the nearest iPad icon or the iPhone / iPod touch iPhone icon to mark PDFs, screenshots and photos, and view the results on your Mac. Press and hold the space bar to view the document immediately, then click the device icon. When both devices are close, click the "Define iPad Tag" icon and select the device. The tool can be highlighted to show that your device is connected.

Use your finger or the Apple Pencil (on iPads that support this feature) to start writing, drawing, or adding shapes. When updating on iPad, iPhone, or iPod touch, you can check for real-time updates on Mac.

Use AirDrop for Mac

With AirDrop, you can easily share files and devices on nearby Mac, iPhone, iPad, and iPod. These devices do not need to share the same Apple ID.

Note: AirDrop for iOS or iPadOS requires the device to have a Lightning or USB-C connector with iOS 7 (or higher) or iPadOS 13 (or higher). Not all older Macs support AirDrop (for a list of supported Macs, see the Apple support article "Using AirDrop on Mac").

Send files from Finder. Hold the Control key and click the item you want to send, select "Share"> "AirDrop", and select the device you want to send to. Or click the Finder icon in the Dock, and click the AirDrop in the left-hand bar (or select "Go"> "AirDrop"). When someone wants to send a file from a window, drag the file from the desktop or another Finder window into them. When you send a file to someone, the recipient can choose whether to accept that file.

Send files from the app. When using an application such as "Page" or "Preview", click the "Share" button, select "AirDrop", and then select the device you want to send to.

Control who can use AirDrop to send you emails. Click the "Control Center" icon in the menu bar, click "AirDrop", and then click "Everyone". You can turn on and off AirDrop here. The iPad, iPhone, and iPod touch have similar settings. Please refer to Apple's support article "How to adjust AirDrop settings".

Tip: If you cannot see the recipient in the AirDrop window, please make sure both devices have AirDrop and Bluetooth turned on and are 9 meters from each other. If the recipient is using an older Mac, try clicking on "Can't find the person you're looking for?".

Use AirDrop to find items. When someone uses AirDrop to send you something on your Mac, you can choose whether to receive it and save it. If you see an AirDrop notification and need an item, click "Accept" and choose to save it in the "Downloads" folder or an application similar to "Photos". If you use the same iCloud account to access multiple devices, you can easily send an item (for example, a photo from an iPhone) from one device to another and save it automatically.

Share the password stored on the iCloud key. In Safari, you can use AirDrop to cut account secret code with contact or another Mac, iPhone, iPad, or iPod touch. From the Safari menu, open "Preferences"> "Passwords", select the website you want to share your password with, and hold the Ctrl key and click. Select "Share AirDrop", then select the person or device in the AirDrop window to share the password.

Phone calls and text messages on Mac

You can answer and make calls directly from the Mac mini. (External microphone required. Accessories are sold separately at Apple.com, your local Apple Store, or other retailers.) You may receive and send messages.

Note: To make or receive calls on a Mac mini, a Wi-Fi connection is required.

Set up FaceTime for the phone. For iPhone, go to "Settings"> "Phone" and enable Wi-Fi hits on iPhone (iOS 9 or later). After that, on your Mac, go to FaceTime> "Preferences", select "Settings", and then click "Call from iPhone". See the Apple support article "Set iPhone and Mac to make calls."

Answer or make calls. When someone calls your iPhone, click the notification displayed on the Mac mini screen. If you don't install the headset, the Mac mini becomes a hands-free phone. To make a call on a Mac, open FaceTime and enter a phone number. Or, in "Contacts", click the phone icon in the FaceTime line as a contact. You can also click on the phone number in Spotlight search or in apps such as Safari or Calendar (iPhone or iPad with mobile connection must be nearby). Please refer to the "FaceTime User Guide" to make a call from the Mac app.

Tip: Temporarily turn off notifications about calls, messages, etc. On your Mac, please turn on the "Do Not Disturb" feature. Click the "Control Center" icon in the menu bar, then click "Do Not Disturb" and select a time limit.

Send and receive messages. Use iMessage to send unlimited messages to friends using Macs, iOS devices, iPadOS, and Apple Watch devices. Send and receive SMS or MMS messages directly from Mac mini. When friends and family send messages to you, you can use a nearby device to reply. All messages will be displayed on Mac mini, iPhone, iPad, iPod touch, and Apple Watch. (Voice messages require an external microphone. Accessories are sold separately at Apple.com, your local Apple Store, and other retailers.) Please refer to this message.

Use the Apple Watch to unlock Mac and enable tasks

If you're wearing your Apple Watch, you can use it to automatically unlock your Mac mini and enable authentication functions, such as entering passwords, unlocking notes and preferences, and authorizing installation without typing a password. These features use strong encryption to provide secure connections between Apple Watch and Mac mini.

To use the automatic opening and approval of the Apple Watch feature, do the following:

- Use the same Apple ID to sign in on Mac and Apple Watch.
- Make sure the Apple Watch is turned on and uses watchOS 3 or higher to unlock Mac automatically; watchOS 6 or higher is required to approve the authentication request.
- Turn on two-factor authentication (see below).

Set up two-factor verification in your Apple ID. To turn on two-factor authentication, go to Apple menu> System Preferences> Apple ID> Password and Security, and choose to set both authentications.

Make sure "Disable auto-login" is also selected. (If you are using FileVault, you will not see this option, but you can still use the "Auto Unlock" and "Approve via Apple Watch" features. For details on FileVault, see File Encryption for Mac with VaVava in macOS User Guide Data.)

Set default unlock. Sign in to all devices with the same Apple ID, then open "System Favorites" on the Mac mini. If your Apple Watch has watchOS 6 installed, click "Security and Privacy", then click "General" and select "Use Apple Watch to open apps and Mac." If your Apple Watch has watchOS 3 to watchOS 5 installed, please select "Allow Apple Watch to unlock Mac". Unless you have watchOS 6 or higher, you cannot authorize authentication activities.

Note: These functions will only work if your Apple Watch has passed password verification. Every time you install your Apple Watch, you need to authorize it, so you do not need to take any further steps after entering the password.

Skip login. Install the guaranteed Apple Watch on your wrist, go to the sleeping Mac mini, and press the key to wake up the Mac. Apple Watch can unlock your Mac for normal operation.

Enable the use of the Apple Watch. When prompted to enter a password, double-click the separate button on the Apple Watch to confirm the password on the Mac. You can view passwords in Safari, allow app installation, unlock locked notes, etc. (WatchOS 6 required). Use the Apple Watch to unlock Mac and enable tasks

Use Apple Pay on Mac

You can use Apple Pay on Mac mini to make easy, secure, and private purchases on the website. With Apple Pay, Apple will never store or share your Apple Card with other credit or bank card information with merchants. If you are using Safari to make online purchases, check out Apple Pay's opt-out option. Use an iPhone or Apple Watch to verify the payment.

Note: Apple Pay and Apple Card are not available in all countries or regions. For details on Apple Pay, please visit "Effortless Cashless". For details about the current issuer, please refer to the Apple Support article for Apple Pay Participating Banks. For information on Apple Card, see Apple Card Support.

Set up Apple Pay. Apple Pay uses an Apple Card or other credit or debit card that you have set on your iPhone or Apple Watch, so no additional settings are required. You must sign in to an iPhone or Apple Watch with the same Apple ID set with Apple Pay and used it on the Mac mini. The default payment card, shipping, and contact details you set up on your iPhone or Apple Watch will be used for purchases on your Mac.

Use an iPhone or Apple Watch to purchase. Click the Apple Pay button on the website and confirm payment, using Face ID, Touch ID, or iPhone passcode, or double-click a separate button on the unlocked Apple Watch. You must sign in to an iPhone or Apple Watch with the same Apple ID set with Apple Pay and used it on the Mac mini.

Note: If you did not choose to set up Apple Pay when you start your Mac mini, you can set it up later in the "Wallet and Apple Pay" "System Preferences" panel. Manage your Apple Card and other payment cards here add or remove cards and update contact details.

Fast hotspot on Mac

Lost Wi-Fi connection? With Instant Hotspot, you can use Personal Hotspot on your iPhone or iPad to connect your Mac mini to the Internet instantly - without a password.

Note: "Personal Hotspot" requires iPhone with iOS 8 (or higher) or iPad mobile with iPadOS 13 (or higher). Please refer to Apple's support article "How to set up a personal hotspot on an iPhone or iPad".

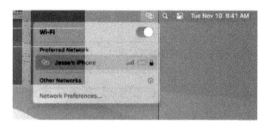

Connect to the device's hotspot. Click the Wi-Fi status icon in the menu bar, then click the link icon next to the iPhone or iPad list (if you don't see the list, click another network). The Wi-Fi icon in the toolbar changes to the "link" icon. You do not need to do anything on the device — the iMac mini will connect automatically.

Tip: If you are asked to enter a password, make sure the device is set correctly. See Apple's support article "Using Instant Hotspot" to connect to your "Personal Hotspot" without entering a password.

Check the connection status. Check the Wi-Fi status menu for mobile signal strength.

If you do not use the hotspot, the Mac mini will disconnect to save battery life.

Use AirPlay for Mac

Use AirPlay screen view to show everything on a Mac mini on the big screen. To make a Mac mini screen on a TV screen or use HDTV as a second display, connect the HDTV to an Apple TV and make sure Apple TV and Mac mini are on the same Wi-Fi network. You can also play online videos directly on HDTV without displaying desktop content, which is great for you if you want to play movies but doesn't work in public.

Use the screen display to emulate your desktop. Click the "Control Center" icon in the menu bar, click "Screen Mirroring", and then click "Apple Mirror". When AirPlay is enabled, the icon becomes blue.

Note: If your Mac supports the AirPlay screen view, when Apple TV and Mac are on the same network, you will see an AirPlay status icon in the menu bar of your Mac. See Use AirPlay play video or mimic the device screen.

In some cases, you can use AirPlay displays even if you are not on the same Wi-Fi network as the Apple TV (also known as your peer AirPlay). To use peer-to-peer AirPlay, you need an Apple TV with tvOS 7.0 or higher (third-generation rev A, model A1469 or higher).

Play web videos without showing off the desktop. When you find a web video with an AirPlay icon, click on the icon, then select your Apple TV.

Tip: If the image does not fit your HDTV screen when viewing the screen, please adjust the desktop size to get the best picture. Click the AirPlay icon in the video and select the option under "Match Desktop Size".

Apple TV is sold separately at Apple.com, your local Apple Store, or other retailers.

Learn more. To learn more about AirPlay, see "Use AirPlay to stream content on your Mac to HDTV" in the macOS user guide. To learn more about using the second display on a Mac mini, see Connect the display on a Mac mini. To resolve the issue, please refer to the Apple support article If AirPlay or Screen Mirroring is not available on your device.

Use AirPrint on Mac

You can use AirPrint wireless to print at:

- Printers are powered by AirPrint on Wi-Fi networks
- Network printer or shared printer for another Mac over Wi-Fi network
- The printer is connected to the USB port of the AirPort base station

Print and print for AirPrint. When you print from the app, click on the "Printer" menu from the "Print" dialog box, then select the printer from the "Nearby Printers" list.

Can't find the printer you want? Make sure you connect it to the same Wi-Fi network as the Mac mini. If you are connected but still do not see it, try adding it: open System Preferences, click Printers & Scanners and click the Apply button. (You may need to temporarily connect the printer to the Mac mini using a USB cable.)

FELIX O. COLLINS

Apps

Stock

The Stocks app is the best way to track a market on a Mac. View prices in the custom clocks, click on stocks to see detailed details and interactive charts and learn about driving trends with news from Apple News.

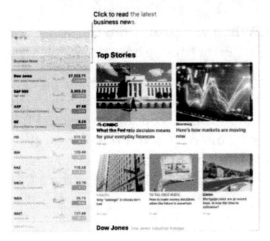

Note: Apple News news and popular news are available in the United States, Canada, the United Kingdom, and Australia. Yahoo has provided news reports from other countries and regions.

Customize your watch list. To add a stock to the watch list, enter the company name or stock code in the "Search" field, hold the Control key and click the stock in search results, then click "Add to Watch List". To remove stock, hold down the control button and click the stock icon, then click "Remove from watch list". You can also hold the Control key and click to open stock on a new tab or window.

Check for market changes. When viewing the watch list, click the green or red button under each price to rotate between price changes, percentage changes, and market value. The watch list includes color-coded sparkles that can track results throughout the day.

Read articles about the companies you follow. Click on the watch list to view interactive charts and other detailed information, and read the latest news about the company.

understand deeply. Want to see what the market was doing last week, last month, or last year? Click the button at the top of the chart to change the time range and view the price in your favorite view.

Your watch list for all devices. When signing in with the same Apple ID, keep a watch list compatible with all devices.

Tip: Click on "Business News" at the top of the watch list to view a collection of timely business articles selected by Apple News.

TV

Watch all your movies and TV displays in the Apple TV app. Buy or rent movies and TV shows, subscribe to channels, and stop and watch from any device.

Start watching now. In "Watch Now", browse the selected feed options based on the channels you've subscribed to and the movies or TV shows you've watched.

Keep watching Next. In "Next", you'll find movies or TV shows you watch, as well as movies and TV shows added to the line. To add a new movie or TV program to "Next", click the "Add to Next" button.

Find out more about movies, TV shows, and kids. To find specific content, click the "Movies", "TV shows" or "kids" tab in the menu bar, and scroll through.

Buy, rent or subscribe. If you find a movie or TV program you want to watch, you can choose to buy or rent it. The channel you subscribe to use on all devices, and up to 6 family members can be used for family sharing.

Choose something from your library. Click on the media library to watch all the movies and TV shows you have purchased or downloaded, categorized. To start watching, just click on a movie or TV game.

Email

Email enables you to manage all email accounts from a single app. It can be used with popular email services such as iCloud, Gmail, Yahoo Mail, and AOL Mail.

One-stop email. Tired of accessing multiple websites to check your email account? Use all accounts to set up email so you can view all your mail in one place. Select "Mail > Add Account".

Get the right message. Type in the search field to see suggestions for messages similar to your query.

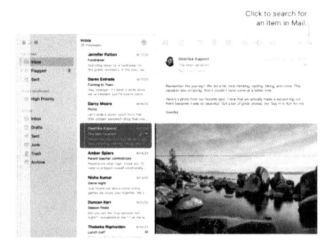

Focus on the essentials. View only the messages you want to see in your inbox. You can block messages from specific senders in the following ways: move them directly to "Trash", mute the active email thread, and then unsubscribe directly from the Email list.

Enter events and contacts directly from Mail. When you receive a message containing an email address or a new event, simply click "Add" to add it to "Contacts" or "Calendar".

Personalize any message. Just click to add an emoji or image. Select a photo from the photo library, or take a photo on your iPhone or iPad. You can also add graphics to your iPhone or iPad. To learn more about importing images and graphics from other devices, see Continuity Camera on Mac and Continuity Sketch and Continuity Markup on Mac.

View fullscreen. When you use "Mail" on the full screen, a new mail window will automatically open in "Split View" on the right, so you can quote other emails in your inbox when you compose an email. Please see the Apple Support article Using two Mac apps next to Split View.

Don't miss the email. Check the "Mail" icon in the Dock to see the number of unread messages. When you receive a new email, a notification will also be displayed at the top right of the screen so you can preview the incoming message. (Don't need notifications? To turn off notifications, open "System Preferences" and click "Notifications.")

Map

Use maps or satellite imagery to get directions and view places. Get the best in town tips from Apple's carefully selected guide.

Explore new places with your guide. To help you find the best places to eat, shop, and explore the world, the map offers selected guides provided with trusted products and partners. You can keep these guidelines and update them as new locations are added.

Create your guide. You can create your guide to your favorite places and share them with friends and family. To create a guide, move the cursor over the "My Guides" in the sidebar, click the "Add" icon to the right, then Hold Control and click the new guide to see the options menu.

3D test. Click the "Looking Around Binoculars" icon to browse the selected city in 3D and cross the streets smoothly in a connected way.

View internal maps of major locations. Find your way out near certain airports and major shopping malls. Just zoom in to see restaurants near your door, find toilets, arrange a meeting place with friends at the mall, and more.

Take public transportation to get there. The map provides details of the public transportation of a particular city. Click the destination bar in the sidebar, and then click the navigation icon to get the suggested route and estimated travel time.

Scheduling an electric car ride becomes easier. Install your electric car on your iPhone, the map will show the location of the charging station along the route, and the charging time will be taken into account when calculating ETA.

Plan your bike route. The map gives you the information you need to plan your bike ride, such as altitude, traffic conditions, and whether there are small slopes. After planning your trip, you can send it to your iPhone.

Get real-time ETA updates. When friends and family members share their estimated time of arrival with you, a map can show you where they are on the route.

Warning: For important information about roaming and to avoid potential interference, please refer to your Mac's safety features.

Tip: To view traffic, click the "View" menu in the menu bar, then select "Show Traffic".

Imovie

With iMovie, you can convert home videos into beautiful movies and Hollywood styles, which can be shared with just a few clicks.

Import video. Import videos from existing media files to iPhone, iPad or iPod touch, camera or Mac. The movie makes you a new library and events.

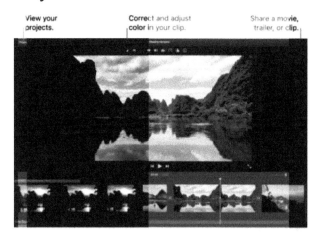

Create a trailer with Hollywood style. Make smart trailers with bright graphics and flying songs. Just add photos and video clips and customize subtitles. First, click the "New" button, click "Trailer", select a template from the "Trailer" window, and then click "Create". Insert characters and subtitles on the "Framework" tab, then add your photos and videos to the "Summary" tab.

Tip: Using portable devices to shoot videos may produce unstable effects, but you can stabilize the video to make the play smoother. Select a clip from the timeline, click the "Stable" button, and then click "Stable Shaking Video".

Home

With the Home app, you can easily and securely control all HomeKit accessories from your Mac.

Controlling accessory. Attachments are displayed as tiles with symbols in the home app. Click the accessory button to control the light and turn off the lights, lock or open doors, view live cameras, etc. You can also adjust the light intensity or temperature of the thermostat. A new feature that appears at the top of the Home app shows a summary of attachments that require your attention or share important status changes.

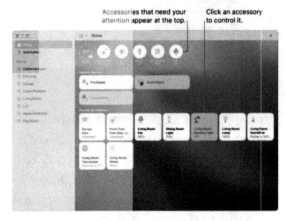

Shared access. You can share the house with your family or guests so they can use the home app to control accessories on their Apple devices.

Create a group. Create a group so that your accessories can be used with a single command. For example, make a good nightclub, if you open it at night, it will turn off all the lights, turn off the shadows and lock the door. To create a group, click, and then click Apply Status.

HomeKit security video. Define active areas within camera view to capture video or receive notifications only when motion is detected in these areas. In addition to human, animal, and car detection, face recognition can also allow security cameras and door locks to identify the people you mark in the "Photos" or "Home" app as recent visitors. (HomeKit Secure Video requires a Family Center and a compatible iCloud program. For more information, see the Home User Guide

Changing lighting. Set up your smart bulb to automatically adjust its color temperature throughout the day to increase comfort and productivity. Get up with warm colors, focus and use cool colors to remind you during the day, and eliminate blue light at night to reduce stress. (Adjusting light requires a home hub. For more information, see Configuring a Router on a Mac for Home Use in the Home User Guide.)

Find my

Use "I Found" to find your friends, family, and Apple devices - all in the same app.

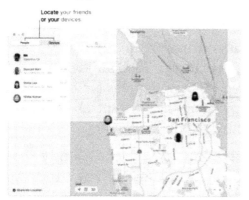

Note: The "I found" feature is not available in all regions or languages.

Share location with friends. In the "People" list, click "Share my location" to tell friends and family your location. You can share location information for an hour, a day, or indefinitely, and you can stop sharing at any time. You can also ask to follow friends so you can see their location on the map and find their location step by step.

Set location alarms. When you arrive or leave a place, automatically send a notification to your friends. Set notifications when friends leave and arrive. When your friend creates alerts about your location, you can view all the notifications by clicking on one "Me" in the "People" list and then scrolling to "Notifications about you"

Protect lost equipment. Use "Find Me" to locate and protect a lost Mac, iPhone, iPad, iPod touch, Apple Watch, or AirPods. Click the device in the device list to find it on the map. Click the Details icon to play audio on the device to help you find it, mark the device as missing so that other people can access your personal information, and you can wipe the device remotely.

Find devices even when they are offline. When my device is not connected to Wi-Fi or a mobile network, "Find Me" will use the Bluetooth signals of other nearby Apple devices to locate your device. These symbols are anonymous and encrypted, helping to recover a lost device without compromising privacy.

Find devices for family members. If you are in the "Family Sharing" group and your family members are sharing their location with you, you can use "Find Me" to help find family member devices.

FaceTime

Use FaceTime to make video and audio calls from your Mac to friends or a group of friends. (FaceTime requires an external camera and microphone. Accessories are sold separately at apple.com, your Apple store, or other retailers.)

Call with FaceTime. Connect the camera and microphone to the Mac mini to make FaceTime video calls. Enter the name, phone number, or email address of the person you want to call, and then click the "Video" button next to their name or number. If it is wrong to make a video call, please click the "Audio" button to make a pure audio call. After receiving a FaceTime invitation, you can choose to join the video only, join the audio, or join both at the same time.

Tip: During a video call, you can drag a small photo-image window to any corner of the FaceTime window.

The FaceTime window shows you how to make a video or audio call, use the search field to enter or search for contact details, and view a list of recent calls.

Use FaceTime with groups. You can talk to up to 32 people. To create a group, enter the name, phone number, or email address of the first contact in the search field, press Enter, and do the same for each contact. Click "Audio" or "Video" at the bottom of the screen to start the call.

Sign language recognition. FaceTime will detect when a participant uses sign language and make that person stand out on the FaceTime team call.

Call. If your iPhone is running iOS 8 or later, please use FaceTime to make calls with your Mac. Just make sure your Mac and iPhone are logged in with the same Apple ID account, and both are enabled features. (On Mac, open FaceTime, select "FaceTime"> "Preferences," and then select "Calls from iPhone.")

Note: Mac mini and iPhone must be connected to the Internet and the same Wi-Fi network to make or receive calls on Mac. To make or receive calls on a Mac mini, an external microphone is required.

The app store

Search the App Store to find and download apps, and get the latest updates for apps.

Get a perfect application. Do you know exactly what you want? Enter the name of the application in the search field and press Return. The apps you download from the App Store will automatically appear on the launchpad. If you click on the "Categories" tab in the sidebar, you can also find new Safari extensions that can add value to your personal browsing experience.

Note: Apple Arcade is not available in all countries or regions.

You only need an Apple ID. To download the free app, please sign in with your Apple ID - select "Store"> "Sign In", or click "Sign In" at the bottom of the sidebar. If you do not have an Apple ID, click "Sign in", then click "Create an Apple ID". If you have an Apple ID but have forgotten your password, click "Forgot Apple ID or password?". Replace. You must also set up an account with purchase information to purchase paid apps.

Use iPhone and iPad apps on Mac. Now, most iPhone and iPad apps can be used on Mac mini with an Apple M1 chip. All apps previously purchased for the iPhone and iPad will be shown on the Mac mini with the Apple M1 chip. Search apps in the App Store to see if they're available on Mac.

play games. Click the "Arcade" tab to learn how to sign up for Apple Arcade, find games to play, find games for your favorite Game Center friends, check out your progress, and more. See "Subscribe to Apple Arcade" in the App Store on Mac, Apple Arcade, and Play games on Mac.

Get the latest updates. If you see the badge in the App Store icon in Dock, there is an update available. Click the icon to open the App Store, then click Update in the sidebar.

Picture

Use iCloud photos and images to edit, edit and share your photos and videos, and keep your photo library up-to-date on all devices. "Photos" shows your best photos, and has powerful search options, you can easily find and enjoy your favorite photos. Easy-to-use editing tools allow you to customize photos and videos like a professional.

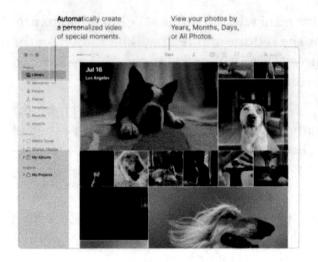

photos on all your devices. With iCloud Photos, you can browse, search, and share all photos and videos on all devices signed in with the same Apple ID. When you take a photo on your iPhone, the photo will be automatically synced to other devices. Additionally, when you edit an image, this setting will be displayed on all devices. First, open "System Favorites", click "Apple ID", then click "iCloud", then select "Photos." To learn more, see the Apple support article "Setting and using iCloud Photos."

Plan as an expert. Create beautiful photos and videos with powerful yet easy-to-use editing tools. Use the edit button above the image or video to enhance it with just one click. To use more powerful editing tools, click "Edit" and use "Smart Slider" to get technical results. You can add filters, rotate, increase exposure, and crop photos and videos.

Change view. "Photos" show the best photos in your photo library, hide duplicates, receipts, and screenshots. Viewing photos of a particular day, month, or year is easier than ever, or click "All Photos" to quickly view your entire collection.

Remember the good times. When you scroll, real-time photos and videos start playing, and your photo library comes alive. Click "Memories" in the sidebar to enable "Photos" to find the best photos and videos and create memorable movies (including music, themes, and transition effects), that you can create and share. You can check the memory on all other devices that use iCloud photos.

Get the perfect lens. Photos can point to objects, groups, and people in your photos and videos. Search for images based on image content, date taken, person by name, captions included, and location (if provided).

People and places. "Photos" understand your photos (including people and what happened to them) and highlight important moments like birthdays, reminders, and travels. Click the "Favorites" button on someone else's photo to make that person a favorite, and that person will always appear at the top of the album. Use the "Places" album to view all photos with location data on the interactive map. Zoom in on a map to show more photos of a particular place.

Tip: You can add location details to any photo. When viewing an image, click the "Info" button, then click "Provide Location" and begin typing. Select a location from the list, or type a location, then press Return.

Use real-time photos to be creative. If you use "Live Photo", you can use the "Loop" effect to continue wrapping the action, or use "Bounce" to play animation back and forth. To look like a professional DSLR camera, use the long exposure to blur the motion in real-time images, and turn ordinary waterfalls or streams into artistic drawings.

Safari

Safari is the fastest and most effective way to browse the web on a Mac. A custom homepage can include your favorite background image and features you want to view, such as "favorites", frequently visited websites, Siri suggestions, your reading list, iCloud tags, and privacy reports. The label now includes an easy-to-identify website icon, and preview when you move the cursor over the label. On supported sites, you can also find the instant translation of websites in other languages.

Note: Not all regions or languages offer translation skills.

Start searching. Start typing in the name or address of the website — Safari will show you similar websites and suggested websites. Or select the items you like or frequently visited on the Safari home page.

Type what you're looking for.

Customize your first Safari page. Your homepage can display "favorites", "realists" items, "privacy reports", etc. You can import a special image to use as a background image, or you can select one of the given backgrounds. Click the "Customize Safari" icon at the bottom right of the home page to set options for the first page.

Get an extension. Extensions add features to Safari to customize your browsing experience. You can find shortcuts and useful information, display news headlines, and instantly share content on your favorite apps and services. The new extension section in the App Store has Safari extensions, which include outstanding editing and popular charts to help you find and download useful items. Please refer to the App Store. After receiving the extension, please open it in Safari preferences. Select the extension tab, then click the check box to open the extension.

View multiple web pages in one window. Click the "Add" button to the right of the tab, or press Command-T to open a new tab and enter an address. To make it easier to use a web page, please drag its tab to the left to adjust it, and save it to the tab bar.

Take a quick look at the contents of the label. An icon (icon or logo associated with a website) on the label allows you to see a web page at a glance. Move the cursor over the tab to see web content previews.

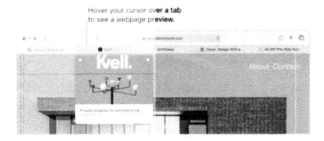

Use strong passwords. When you register a new account on the web, Safari will automatically create and fill in a new password for you. If you choose to use a strong password, the password will be stored on your iCloud key and will be automatically filled in on all devices you sign in with the same Apple ID. Safari securely scans your passwords, identifies any stored passwords that may be involved in infringing data that may be sent, and makes it easier to upgrade to a "Sign in with Apple" account (if available). (See "Sign in with Apple on Mac" in the macOS User Guide.)

Browse the web safely and privately. Safari will warn you if you visit an unsafe website or website that tries to trick you into sharing personal information. By identifying and deleting data left by the tracker, it can automatically protect you from site tracking. Safari will ask for your permission before allowing social networks to view your activities on third-party websites. Safari protects you from web tracking attacks by making it harder for your Mac to identify differently.

View Privacy Report. You can click the "Privacy Report" button on the Safari Toolbar to view site tracking programs where Safari blocks each website, and you can better understand how that website handles your privacy. Click the "Full Report" button to view the privacy statement, which contains detailed information about the website activity tracker.

Translate web (beta) pages. You can instantly translate the entire web page into Safari. If you encounter a Safari which can translate, you will see the translation button in the website address field. Click to translate between the following languages: English, Spanish, Simplified Chinese, French, German, Russian and Brazilian Portuguese. The button changes color to a blue translation icon to display when a web page is translated.

Open image-in-image. When playing a video, click and hold the "Audio" button on the tab, then select "Add Image-to-Image" in the menu below. Your video appears in a floating window, and you can drag and drop a window so you can watch it while performing other tasks on your Mac. You can also set auto-play options in this submenu. To mute the video, click the "Audio" button.

Find answers

macOS User Guide

The macOS User Guide provides more details on how to use the Mac mini.

Get help. Click the Finder icon in the Dock, then click the "Help" menu in the menu bar, then select "MacOS Help" to open the macOS User Guide. Or type a question or word in the search field and select a topic from the results list.

Check the title. To find the topic in the macOS User Guide, you can browse or search. To browse, click "Table of Contents" to see a list of topics, and then click a title to read it. Or type what you want in the search field to get the exact answer.

Learn about new features. Click the "Help" menu and select "See what's new in macOS" to learn more about the latest macOS features.

Tip: If you do not remember the location of the menu item in the app, please search for "Help". Place the cursor on the result and the arrow will show you the command.

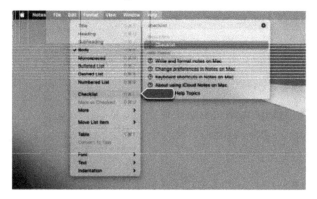

Frequently asked questions about Mac

How can you get Mac mini support? Go for Mac mini support.

I'm new to Mac. Are there any tips for PC users? Yes, that's right! See Apple Support Tips for Mac Tips for Windows Switchers. Check out a quick visit to Mac Basics. You may be interested in keyboard shortcuts on Mac.

How to take a screenshot on a Mac? Press Command-Shift-3 to take a full screenshot. Press Command-Shift-4 to take a screenshot of the selected location on the screen. To learn more, see Taking a screenshot on a Mac.

What is my serial number? Select the "Apple" menu> "About this Mac". The serial number is the last item on the list. You can find the serial number at the bottom of the Mac mini. Please see the Apple support Article Mac mini: How to get a serial number.

How to get Mac mini documents? For the Essentials guide, select the Apple menu> "About this Mac", click the "Support" tab, and then click on "User Manual." On the "Support" tab, you can also click "MacOS Help" to open the app's user guide. For older Mac models, please refer to product browsing manuals.

How can I get help with the app? When using the app, click the "Help" menu in the menu bar at the top of the screen.

What is the security information for the Mac mini? Please see the important Mac security details.

How can you get technical specifications? Go to the specifications of the Mac mini technology, or select Apple Menu> About This Mac, then click the Up button.

How can you check for disk problems? Use Disk Utility. Please refer to the "Disk Utility User Guide" in Disk Utility on Mac to configure storage devices.

How do you reinstall macOS? Use macOS to restore. (The MacOS Mac mini recovery process with Apple M1 chip is different from other Mac mini models.) Please see how you can re-install macOS in macOS recovery.

Note: Starting with macOS Big Sur, Time Machine backups do not include program files. See Back up and Restore the Mac.

What should I do before selling or trading on a Mac? Back up data, and restore Mac to factory settings. Before you sell, offer, or trade your Mac, see what you do.

Keyboard shortcuts for Mac

You can press a combination of keys to perform tasks on the Mac mini you usually use on a trackpad, mouse, or other devices. The following is a list of the most commonly used keyboard shortcuts.

Shortcut	meaning
Commandment-X to the	Cut out the selected item and copy it to the clipboard.
Commandment-C	Copy the selected item to the

pasteboard.

Commandment-V   Paste the clipboard contents into the

current document or

application.

Command-Z   Undo the last command. Press Command-

Shift-Z to reset.

Commandment-A   Select all items.

Command-F   Open the Discover window or search for

items in this docu-

ment.

Command-G   Find the next match for the item you

want.

Press Command-Shift-

G to get the latest

experience.

Command-H   Hide previous app window. Press

Command-Option-H

to view previous

apps, but hide all

other apps.

Command-M   Minimize the front Dock window. Press

Command-Option-M

to minimize all

windows of the previ-

ous application.

Command-N   Open a new document or window.

Command-O   Open the selection of an item or open

a dialog

FELIX O. COLLINS

box to select a file to
open.

Command-p   Print the current document.

Command-S   Keep the current document.

Command-W   Close the front window. Press Command-
                            Option-W to close all
application windows.

Command-Q   Exit the current app.

Command-Option-Esc   Select an application to force quit.

Command-Tab   Switch to the next application use
                            between open ap-
plications.

Command-Shift-5   Turn on screenshot usage. You can
also
                            use the following
shortcuts to take
                            screenshots:

Press Command-Shift-3   Press Command-Shift-4 to take a

to take a full screenshot. screenshot of the selected location
on the
                            screen.

When switching from PC to Mac, check out the Apple Tips Mac
Mac Tips support article for Windows Switcher for a list of Mac
keyboard shortcuts and differences between Mac and Windows
keyboards. For more keyboard shortcuts, check out Apple Keyboard shortcuts.

Security features on Mac mini

Your Mac mini provides the following security features to protect your computer content and to prevent unauthorized software downloads during the launch:

- Safe storage: Mac mini storage drive is encrypted with hardware keys to provide advanced security. In the event of a disastrous failure, data recovery may not be possible, so you need to posterior up your files to an external source. See Apple's support article "About Encrypted Storage on a New Mac". You can set Time Machine or other backup programs to back up your computer regularly. Please refer to the macOS User Guide to use Time Machine to back up files and Apple Support article Use Time Machine to back up your Mac.
- Safe boot and boot utility safe: Safe boot supports automatic unlock. It is designed to ensure that the software installed on the computer was originally powered by Apple. See Apple's support article "About Safe Boot."

If your Mac mini fails to get started by detecting unreliable items, it will open insecure recovery and automatically fix the problem if possible. To learn more about "Starting Security Utility" or to learn how to set up some options (for example, boot from an external device), see the Apple Support Article "About Starting a Security Service."

- System integrity (applies to Apple M1 chip only): The Apple M1 chip is designed to ensure that the macOS software version downloaded at startup is authorized by Apple and continues to secretly protect MacOS established authorization while MacOS is running. This makes it very difficult for malware or malicious websites to take advantage of your Mac.
- Data protection (Apple M1 chip only): In addition to the default drive encryption using the Apple M1 chip on Mac mini, third-party application developers can use advanced file encryption to better protect sensitive data without affecting system performance.

Note: In rare cases, such as a power failure during the MacOS upgrade process, the Mac mini may not respond and may need to restore the firmware to the T2 chip. See Apple support article "Restore or restore Mac firmware to Apple Configurator 2."

Save space on Mac mini

With Backup Setup, you can automatically free up space on your Mac mini by providing files on demand. Your original files will be stored on iCloud and IMAP email or Exchange server, so you can download them at any time. Some tools can identify and delete large files.

Configure storage. To view storage recommendations, go to Apple menu> About this Mac, click Storage, and then click Manage. Depending on how you set up your Mac, you'll see various suggestions. If you do not have enough storage space on your Mac, you will see a warning with a link in the store window.

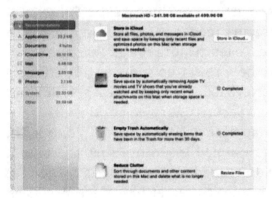

Set options to:

- Save to iCloud: Save all files, photos, and messages to iCloud and save space on your Mac.
  - Desktop and Documents: Save all files in the "Desktop and Documents" folder on Cloud Drive. When storage space is required, Cloud Drive will store newly opened files on Mac and provide older files as needed.

- Photos: Save photos and videos to iCloud photos. When storage space is required, iCloud photos will use advanced types of photos and videos on Mac and provide real-time on-demand.
- Email: Save all emails and attachments to iCloud. When storage space is required, iCloud will store the latest attachments to the Mac and provide the oldest files as needed.

Even if your files are stored in the cloud, they can be accessed from the rest of your Mac mini. See Access your iCloud content on Mac.

- Customize storage: Save space on your Mac by storing movie and TV programs in the Apple TV program. You can choose to automatically delete movies or TV shows on the Mac mini after watching the Mac mini. You can download them again at any time.
- Automatically remove waste: Automatically delete items that have been in the trash for more than 30 days.
- Reduce confusion: easily identify large files and delete unwanted files. To browse large files, click the sidebar - books, documents, iCloud drive, email, messages, create music, photos, dump paper, etc.

To help you save space, MacOS will also do the following:

- Prevent yourself from downloading the same file from Safari twice
- Remember to uninstall the software once you have finished installing the new app
- Clear logs and storage that can be safely removed when storage space is limited

Take a screenshot on a Mac

Browse through the "Screenshot" menu to find all the controls needed to take screenshots and screen videos. You can also take a voice during screen recording. Customized workflow allows you to take photos and videos on screen, and easily share, edit or save them.

Access screen control. Press Command-Shift-5. You can capture the entire screen, the selected window, or part of the window. You can record the entire screen or selected parts of the screen.

Use the icons at the bottom of the screen to capture the selection, the "screen selection option" icon, the recording screen, the "record screen" icon, and more. Click on options to change your storage location, set the timer before shooting, set the microphone and audio options, or display directions. Click Take or Record to take a screenshot or video.

After taking a screenshot or video, an icon will appear in the corner of the screen. Drag the icon to the document or folder, swipe right to save it quickly, or click edit or share.

Note: You can also open the "Screenshot" app from the "Other" folder in the launchpad, or go to the "Applications"> "Applications" folder in Finder.

Tag your screenshot. Click on the screenshot icon to use the marking tool and define it. You can also click the "Share" icon to send a marked screen to colleagues or friends directly from the screen itself. See marking files on Mac in macOS user directory.

Mac resources, services, and support

You can find more details about the Mac mini in system reports, Apple diagnoses, and online resources.

System report. For details on the Mac mini, use "System Report". Indicates which Hardware and software are installed, serial number and operating system type, how much memory is installed To open "System Report", select the "Apple"> "About this Mac" menu, and click on "System Report".

Apple Diagnosis. You can use Apple Diagnostics to help determine if there is a problem with a part of your computers, such as a memory or processor. Apple Diagnostics can help you determine the cause of a potential hardware problem and provide a first step in trying to resolve the problem. If you need further assistance, Apple Diagnostics will also help you contact AppleCare.

Before using Apple Diagnostics, disconnect all external devices, such as hard drives or external displays. Make sure the Mac mini is connected to the Internet.

To start Apple Diagnostics on a Mac mini using the Apple M1 chip, restart the computer, press and hold the power button for 10 seconds to turn on "Startup Options", then press and hold Command-D to enter diagnostic mode. To start Apple Diagnostics on some Mac mini models, restart your computer and hold the D button while you start.

When prompted, select your local language. Press Return or click the right arrow button. The basic test of Apple Diagnostics takes a few minutes to complete. If a problem is found, the description of the problem and other instructions will be displayed. If you need to contact AppleCare, please write down all the reference codes before Apple Diagnostics is out.

Online resources. For online service information and support information, go to "Welcome to Apple Support". You can learn about Apple products, browse online brochures, check for software updates, contact other Apple users, and get Apple's services, support, and advice. For more information on Mac mini, please visit Mac mini support.

AppleCare support. If you need help, and AppleCare representative can help you install and open the app and resolve the issue. Call your nearest help center (free for the first 90 days). If you call, please be prepared for the purchase date and Mac mini serial number.

For a complete list of support phone numbers, please visit the Apple website for assistance and service. Phone numbers can change at any time, and country and home values can be used.

Your 90-day free support starts from the date of purchase.

Safety, handling, and regulatory information

Important Mac security details

Warning: Failure to comply with these security regulations may result in fires, electric shocks, or other damage, or damage to the Mac mini or other equipment. Before using the Mac mini, please read the safety information below.

See. Install the Mac mini in a hard, stable working environment to allow adequate airflow under and inside the computer. Don't put things into souls. If the Mac mini is discarded, burned, punctured or crushed, or mixed with liquids, grease, and lubricant, it may cause damage.

The contact is liquid. Keep the Mac mini away from liquid sources, such as drinks, grease, cosmetics, washbasins, bathtubs, showers, etc. Protect your Mac mini from humid, humid, or humid conditions (such as rain, snow, and fog).

Power. The only way to completely shut off the power is to unplug the power cord. Make sure at least one power cord is easily accessible so you can unplug the Mac mini if needed. If there are any of the following situations, please disconnect the power cord (pull plug, not power cord) and disconnect all cables:

- The power cord or plug is rotten or damaged.
- She poured something into the box.
- Your Mac mini is exposed to extreme rain or moisture.
- Your Mac mini has been canceled, or the case is broken.
- You suspect your Mac mini needs service or repair.
- You want to clear the case (use only the recommended steps, as described later in this document).

Power details:

- Power: 100 to 240 V AC
- Current: Size 2 A
- Frequency: 50 to 60 Hz

Loss of hearing. Listening to high-volume sounds can damage your hearing. The background sound and frequent exposure to high volume can make the sound appear quieter than the actual sound. Only compatible earbuds, earphones, or earpieces can be used with a Mac mini. Before you put anything in your ears, turn on the sound and check the volume. See sounds and hearing.

Warning: To avoid possible hearing damage, do not listen at high volume for too long.

It is being fixed. Your Mac mini does not have easy-to-use components. Do not open or disassemble the Mac mini or try repairing it or installing other items. Unpacking the Mac mini can damage or damage it. If your Mac mini needs repair, damage, malfunction, or liquid contact, please contact Apple or an Apple-approved repair center, such as Apple's authorized service provider. If you try to unlock the Mac mini, you may damage the computer, and the limited warranty for the Mac mini does not cover such damage.

wandering. Maps, directions, and location-based applications depend on the data service. These data services may change and may not be available in all regions, leading to maps, directions, or location-based information that may not be available, accurate, or incomplete. Compare location-based information provided with your location and follow the signals sent to resolve any differences. Do not use these services when performing tasks that require your full attention. When using the navigation area, always follow the included signs and applicable rules and regulations, and use common sense.

Disruption of medical equipment. The Mac mini contains items and radios that output electric fields. These power outages can affect medical devices such as pacemakers and defibrillators. Please consult your physician and medical device manufacturer for specific information on your medical device and whether it is necessary to maintain a safe distance between the medical device and Mac mini. If you suspect the Mac mini is interfering with medical equipment, please stop using the Mac mini.

Medical conditions. If you think your health may be affected by using a Mac mini (for example, fainting, loss of energy, stress, or headache), please consult a physician before using a Mac mini.

Repeat the exercise. When you do repetitive tasks (such as typing or playing games) on your Mac mini, your hands, arms, wrists, shoulders, neck, or other body parts may feel uncomfortable. If you feel unwell, stop using the Mac mini and consult a doctor.

Top jobs. The Mac mini is not suitable for use in areas where computer malfunction can lead to death, personal injury, or serious environmental damage.

Explosions and other atmospheric conditions. It is dangerous to use the Mac mini in any area where there may be a risk of explosion, especially in areas where the air contains a lot of flammable chemicals, vapor, or particles (such as grain, dust, or metal powder). Placing the Mac mini in an area with a lot of industrial chemicals, including molten gases such as helium near vapor, can damage or interfere with the operation of the Mac mini. See all signs and instructions.

Important details for processing Mac

Workplace. The performance of the Mac mini without these layers can affect performance:

- Operating temperature: 10 ° to 35 ° C (50 ° to 95 ° F)
- Storage temperature: -40 ° to 47 ° C (-40 ° to 116 ° F)
- Relative humidity: 5% to 90% (no condensing)
- Performance height: tested, up to 16,404 meters (0 to 5000 meters)

Do not use the Mac mini in areas with too much dust in the air, cigarettes, cigarettes, ashtrays, stoves, or fireplaces, or use unprocessed tap water near an ultrasonic filter. Smoking, cooking, heating, or using small air particles from an ultrasonic humidifier using filtered water can get into Mac mini holes in rare cases.

Manage Mac mini. Before you mount or reset the Mac mini, turn it off and disconnect all cords and cords. Lifting the Mac mini, hold it by its sides.

Use connectors and ports. Do not force the connector into the port. Before installing a power cord in a power port, make sure that the power port is completely free of debris. When connecting the device to the port, make sure that there is no debris in the port, that the connector looks like a port, and that the connector is in a good position relative to the port.

Important: Use only original cords that come with your computer or accessories, or cords sold in Apple stores or online at apple.com.

Save your Mac mini. If you want to keep your Mac mini longer, keep it in a cool place (71 ° F or 22 ° C is best).

Clean Mac mini. When cleaning the outside of the Mac mini and its components, turn off the Mac mini first, then unplug all the power cords and wires. Then apply a soft, clean, damp cloth to wipe the outside of the Mac mini. Avoid getting wet in any openings. Do not spray the liquid directly on the computer. Do not use alcohol, sprays, solvents, abrasives, or cleaners containing hydrogen peroxide, these cleaners may damage the surface of the case.

Clean the display. To clean the display, first, turn off the power on your Mac mini, then unplug all the power cords and cables. Follow the cleaning instructions that come with the monitor.

Accessories such as Magic Mouse 2, Magnet Trackpad 2, Magic Keyboard, and Monitor are sold separately at apple.com or your local Apple Store.

Control Details

The device provides Mac mini control information, certificates, and compliance marks. Select the "Apple" menu> "About This Mac"> "Support"> "Certification Regulatory".

Apple and nature

At Apple, we recognize our responsibility to reduce the environmental impact of our operations and products.

For details, please visit Apple's environmental website.

Information on disposal and reuse

Do not place it in the trash can.

This label means do not dispose of the product and/or battery in the household waste. When you decide to dispose of this product and/or its battery, please dispose of it following local environmental laws and guidelines.

For information on Apple's reuse program, recycling points, blocked items, and other environmental programs, please visit Apple's environmental website.

Details about garbage disposal and recycling

The sign above indicates that the product and/or its battery should not be discarded along with the household waste. If you wish to dispose of this product and/or battery, please dispose of it following local environmental laws and guidelines. For more information about Apple's reuse plans, recycling points, limited features, and other environmental programs, please visit apple.com/us/envelo or apple.com/la/envelo.

Details of Brazil-Disposal and recycling

The sign indicates that this product and/or battery should not be discarded or treated as household waste. When you decide to dispose of this product and/or its battery, please perform faça-o functions locally according to your reading method and specific settings. For details on restricted content or Apple's reuse program, collection points, and information calls, please visit apple.com/br/envelo.

Details of the European Union Disposal

The sign above indicates that according to local laws and regulations, your product and/or battery must be disposed of separately from your home. When the product service life expires, take it to a collection point designated by local authorities. The separate collection and reuse of the product and/or its battery during disposal will help conserve natural resources and ensure that it is reused in a way that protects human health and the environment.

Tips and tricks

How to sign a document digitally

Since most of us work from home, signing documents on a Mac is more important than ever. However, there is a much easier way than to print a document, sign it, and then scan it back to Mac.

Open preview, then click Tools> Annotation> Signature> Manage signatures in the menu bar. In the pop-up box, click Create Signature. You can now use the trackpad or iPhone to sign, or you can use the Mac camera to capture your signature on paper. To sign a document at any time, simply open it in "Preview", then click "Tools"> "Comment"> "Sign", and then click your signature to replace it.

How to customize the Finder sidebar

Default file finder for MacOS. It is very customizable and can meet your needs with just a few clicks. For example, if you have a frequently accessed folder, you can add it to the Finder sidebar for quick access. Just go to the folder and click and drag it to the sidebar. For applications, press and hold the Cmd key, then drag its icon upwards. You can delete items using the sidebar tab in Finder> Preferences.

Additionally, you can change the buttons displayed above the Finder window. Click the View> Customize toolbar, and then insert, remove or rearrange the buttons as needed.

How to rename a filegroup in Finder

Apple makes it easy to rename file groups on MacOS, but if you need more control, you can use many advanced options. First, select all the files you want to rename, then hold Cmd and click on them, then click "Rename x items" (where x is the number of selected files).

A pop-up window with various options will appear. You can choose to rename a file by entering the current file name, entering text to the end of the file name, or renaming the file depending on various features such as file name and date. You can also use the word library. At the bottom of the pop-up window preview, to see what the renamed file looks like.

How to use the writing pad

Do you want to use the file as a template for the following texts? There is a good way called a "stationery pad" that can accomplish difficult tasks.

Find the file you need to use as a template, then hold the Ctrl key and click on it, then click "Get Info". Here, check the box "Stationery Pad". Now, every time you double-click this file, macOS will present you with a copy of the original file, allowing you to make changes without changing the template document.

How to use space on multiple desktops

Do you like to keep work and play separately? Use space. The best function of macOS is to allow you to have multiple desktops, each opening different windows, and files. It works well when you need to separate projects and focus on one project at a time.

To open the "Space" menu, swipe up the trackpad with four fingers, press the "Mission Control" button, or press the Ctrl + Up arrow. Click the "+" icon to add a new desktop. Use the four fingers to slide or press the Ctrl + left arrow or the Ctrl + right arrow to navigate between desktops. To move a file or window to another desktop, click and drag it to the top of the screen until the "Space" menu appears, then drop it to your favorite desktop.

How to place shortcuts in window corners

Windows 10 has a Peek, when your mouse moves to the bottom right corner of the eye, it will display the desktop for a while. macOS has a better "hot corner" function, allowing users to assign controls to each corner of the screen.

Launch System Preferences> Appliance Control> Hot Restaurants. Here, you can select the action in each corner, including the

"Notification Center" display, screen lock, start screen saver, and so on. You can add keys to the mix, or you can assign the same action to multiple corners at the same time

How to use Mac window aperture capabilities

Resizing the window may seem easy - you just need to click and drag the corner of the window, easy? But in macOS, you'll find some nice additional options.

When resizing a window, hold down the Shift key and it will maintain its current size. Hold the Alt key at the same time, and the size of one side or corner will be equal to the side that changed your size. Hold down the Shift and Alt key at the same time to use this setting two workers at the same time.

How to share contact details between contacts

By using the "Contacts" app, users can share their personal information with others, but sometimes you may need to send certain information, such as your work email address instead of your home street address.

To do this, you first need to define your card by selecting it in "Contacts" and then clicking on "Card" > "Set this card as my card". Now, open the "Contacts" preferences and click on the "Cards" tab, then check the "Enable My Private Card" box. Click "Edit" on the card, then uncheck the boxes next to any items you do not want to share, then click "Finish."

How to add spacers to the base

You only need to use a few last commands to install certain pads in Mac's Dock, which gives you a new option for how to edit app icons. Open the Terminal from Go > Utilities, then type the following: "kill all Dock", then press Return (this command is critical).

The base will disappear and reappear with a spacer on the right. Type "exit" in Terminal, then press Return, then exit Terminal. Now, you can drag interval tiles to any position in the Dock. Repeat any number of shims.

How to unlock Mac with Apple Watch

A good example of how the Apple ecosystem works to set up an Apple Watch to unlock a Mac. When both devices are signed with the same Apple ID, you just need to press any button to activate your Mac, and your watch will turn on automatically.

To set this feature, launch "System Preferences" and click "Security and Privacy". Check the box next to using your Apple Watch to unlock apps with your Mac (you may be asked to enter your Mac password). If you are using macOS Catalina and watchOS 6, this can be used elsewhere when typing a Mac password.

How to transfer files quickly

When you press and hold the "T" when the Mac is turned on, you can enter the specified disk mode. In this mode, use Thunderbolt 3 cables to quickly transfer large files between two Macs.

Paste method using style matching

When pasting content, if you use Option-Shift-Command-V instead of Command-V, you can convert the attached content to an existing content style in the text. For example, if you have a section of text in italics, and you want to attach text to the web and make it italic, you can use this keyboard shortcut.

How to turn a website into a dock application

You can add any website to the port by dragging the URL bar at the bottom of the dock containing open and recently used applications. Adding a website to the port can make it start faster because you can click on that location next to all apps.

How to print quickly

If you want to "Printers and Scanners" section of "System Choices" and slog the icons of your preferred printers to the desktop, you can drag and drop files to printer images to print them automatically.

How to share the screen in messages

In a message chat with someone, click the "Details" link, then click the dual-looking icon to start sharing the screen with the person you're chatting with. If you can let them click on the screen sharing option, you can easily help those family members who are less tech-savvy to solve problems.

How to preview files from Dock

In the "Downloads or Documents" folder in Dock, hover your mouse over the file and press the space bar to preview it. This also applies to selected files in Finder.

How to check file storage location

If there is a Download or Documents folder in the port, you can hold Command and click on a folder or file to show where it is in Finder.

How to move files quickly

To use keyboard shortcuts to move files from one place to another, simply use Command-C to copy the files you want to move, and then use Option-Command-V to move those files to another location.

How to use Spotlight for search

To launch a search interface that lets you find files on your Mac, just use Command + Space. From finding files to answering basic questions to solving mathematical problems, Spotlight can accomplish a variety of things.

How to switch between apps

To switch between using applications, press command + Tab. Continue to hold the Command key, then press the Tab key to rotate through open applications. Release when the desired program is highlighted.

How to close an application from the app switch

In Command + Tab view, press the Q button while holding Command to close the open application.

www.ingramcontent.com/pod-product-compliance
Lightning Source LLC
LaVergne TN
LVHW051706050326
832903LV00032B/4040